Jesus is Our Example

ISBN:978-1-950252-05-3

Jesus is Our Example

By Summer McClellan

Other books

by Summer McClellan

The Impossible Marriage

Grace, What is It?

Faith, What is It?

Passing the Tests of Life

Satan Has No Power Over You, You Belong to Jesus Now

For to this you were called, because Christ also suffered for us, leaving us an example, that you should follow His steps

1 Peter 2:21

To Jim

You walk in humility.

Contents

Preface

This book came from an aversion I had to a certain scripture. A scripture which has since become my favorite scripture. Here it is...

Servants be submissive to your masters with all fear, not only to the good and gentle, but also to the harsh. For this is commendable, if because of conscience towards God one endures grief and suffering wrongfully. For what credit is it if, when you are beaten for your faults, you take it patiently? But when you do good and suffer for it, if you take it patiently, this is commendable before God. For to this you were called, because Christ also suffered for us, leaving us an example, that you should follow His steps: Who committed no sin, nor was any guile found in His mouth, who, when He was reviled did not revile in return; when He suffered, He did not threaten, but committed Himself to Him who judges righteously. 1 Peter2:18-23

I hated this scripture. I really hated this scripture. Be submissive to someone who is mistreating you. No way! If I am submissive and endure grief and suffering wrongfully, then it is commendable before God? Big deal! That kind of suffering for just being commendable? I just didn't get it. It sounded like a raw deal anyway you looked at it, if you were patient or if you weren't.

Then I realized something. We all get raw deals in our lives sometime or another. It happens.

I thought of a man I knew who lost his life savings

when the investor he invested with squandered his money. He never got over it. He died bitter. We all get bad situations that we don't deserve. It is bound to happen. This man I knew, he did not know how to handle it. He became so bitter. I believe it is why he died. I thought about it, this was severe; this man, I knew lost all his money. How can he overcome that? I realized the answer was in this scripture! We are to take wrongdoings patiently, and we are to commit ourselves to Him who judges righteously. I realized because Jesus did it, that's why we can. Jesus was tortured, mocked, spit on, He had his beard pulled out, He was whipped, stripped and crucified. He took it patiently and He committed Himself to Him who judges righteously. And He was totally innocent. That is why we can do it. That is how we can do it, because Jesus did it. He became our example, and we can follow His steps.

Then I realized that is how Jesus defeated Satan! Jesus overcame evil, and this is the way He did it. We face the same devil that Jesus did. He is looking to destroy us just like he tried to destroy Jesus, but instead Jesus won! This man I knew, who lost his money, was overcome by evil, the devil, but he could have beat the devil like Jesus did, by doing what Jesus did. Suddenly I loved this verse. I love, love, love this verse! It is the answer! It is how we overcome in our life. We follow our example JESUS!!!!!

I started reading the gospels again and I realized something! We are not following Jesus' example. I studied His words. I realized I wasn't living this stuff; I had a long way to go. Christianity suddenly looked very different. Jesus did not lay out an easy path. He gave us an example that goes against everything we know. Now I wanted to really look at just what Jesus' example really was all about. I wanted to see what the Bible was really saying. I wanted to follow it.

And my attitude changed about it being commendable before God. What greater thing could we accomplish, not only in this life but the one to come, to be commendable before God. His rewards are out of this world, not only in heaven but in the here and now. God showed me if we follow Jesus steps, and we commit ourselves to Him like Jesus did, when we are mistreated or suffer loss, that everything taken from us will be restored. We overcome the enemy. We win! This entire book is based on this one scripture that I used to hate, about Jesus being our example, and about us following His steps. This is the answer. I don't hate this stuff anymore; it is so exciting! I want to learn more about Jesus, how He lived and what He taught, and I want to follow His example. Please read on.

Chapter One

Jesus Values People

Therefore, be followers of God as dear children. And walk in love, as Christ also has loved us and given Himself for us, an offering and a sacrifice to God for a sweet-smelling aroma. Ephesians 5:1-2

When I was a teenager, back in the 1970's, we had a little old white-haired minister visit our town. His name was Eddie Walker. I first heard about him from my mother. My parents got home extremely late, about four in the morning. They had been to their Christian dinner club.

"Why in the world did you come home so late?" I

asked.

"We had a little old man for the speaker," my mom told me. "He was absolutely incredible; he was a saint, like meeting Moses or something. He would not finish the meeting until he had prayed for every person there."

I was intrigued. I found out he was going to have another meeting in town. So, I decided to go. It was one of the most amazing experiences of my life. The meeting was in an old house that was converted into a coffee house. It didn't accommodate too many people, maybe seventy-five. Eddy sang a few songs and began to talk. He was a short little man. He had a wooden leg, and he was soft spoken. But the most amazing thing about him was his eyes; they shone with love.

The things Eddy said were amazing. I immediately saw what my mother meant when she said he was like meeting Moses. That was just what it was like in Eddy's meetings. It was like someone had come from heaven and was here in the room, a saint. He was in communication with God all through the meeting. He would tell us what God was saying. At one point he said there were five people in the room that God was going to anoint for a special ministry.

He knew God so intimately. He talked about his conversations with Jesus. He told how he was taking a morning walk and praying. He told the Lord, "It is such a beautiful morning."

Eddy said the Lord replied, "I want to show you another beautiful morning." Then he said everything around him disappeared. He was standing in another time. He knew it was ancient Jerusalem. The people on the street were saying, "They are going to crucify Jesus today."

Eddy was there. I don't know how, but he was there. He saw Jesus crucified. He said he was so close he could have reached out and touched the cross. He saw Jesus' mother crying. He witnessed everything, he watched as Jesus died and the soldier pierced his side. I had never heard of such a thing. Did he actually go back in time? I had never heard of someone having such experiences with God. I never had seen anyone with this level of relationship with God before.

He continued to amaze us as he then told how God showed him the day that He created the world! Eddie actually got to witness this event! God creating the world!!!!This man had a close walk with the Lord! This was my kind of meeting; I could have stayed forever listening to this man!

Then Eddy began to pray for people. He would point to someone and call them up. Then the person he called up front would stand before him. He would look into their eyes, sometimes he would cry and sometimes he would laugh. He would seem to know what was inside them. He would tell people things, messages from God or something from their past that God wanted to heal them from. It was obvious the people were being greatly impacted. Some would double over and cry. Almost always before he was done, they would fall on the floor. He took his time with each one. Eddy stopped praying and looked at us, his amazed captive audience. He told us, "Each person I pray for is like a present from God to me. God shows me inside each person."

That is exactly what it seemed like when he prayed for each person, like he was getting a present. As he would gaze into each person's eyes, his delight would grow and the love and emotion he had for each person would bubble over.

He was not in a hurry; he took his time with each one. Eddie was thoroughly enjoying himself. Sometimes as he prayed for a person, he would whisper something in their ear, and they would double over crying with emotion. Then "Bam" power would hit them, the power of God. Most would immediately fall to the floor, enraptured in glory. I was sitting close to the front. I could see Eddy as he was looking in their eyes, he was seeing deep within each one.

Summer Learns the Value of People Watching Eddy

I was learning something that night that I have never forgotten; the value of each person to God, and to Eddy. You see I had just turned seventeen at the time of this meeting. I was like a lot of rotten teenagers. I was very self- centered. I thought of some people as important and other people as not important. I had seen many of the people in this crowd before at other Christian meetings in town. There were in this meeting a group of older ladies, which I would see at the old-fashioned Pentecostal church in our town. That's where the older crowd went. I would only visit there if they had a good speaker. Those ladies got on my nerves. To my seventeen-year-old mind they were older than the hills, very overweight and always crying. I saw them as unimportant and annoying. I didn't think Eddy would bother with them, I thought he would just want to pray with my "happening" younger on fire for the Lord crowd, because we were cool, and I couldn't wait for Eddy to call me to the front and pray for me.

He pointed at an extremely heavy older lady; I had seen before but didn't think twice about her. He called her up to him. He looked at her like the most precious treasure on earth. He held her hands and looked into her eyes; it seemed he took on her pain. He moaned and cried, and they cried together. He was in no hurry to move onto someone else. His eyes looked like deep pools of love as he ministered to this woman. Then he pointed to another woman, he seemed to be picking those that no one else would. He would love them and whisper to them. Whatever it was he said they would break down with emotion. Then they would fall to the floor, what we Pentecostals call "slain in the Spirit".

Finally, he pointed to me. When I got up there my heart was pounding in excitement. He whispered to me that I was one of the five that God had a special anointing to give me for a special ministry. That was the last thing I knew before I seemed to float to the floor in a wonderful cloud of ecstasy. I felt like I was enveloped in a cloud. I didn't feel the floor when I hit it. It felt like I landed in a cloud of feathers. I never felt the power of the Holy Spirit on me so strong. I live for this stuff. I felt like I was floating on clouds. I was living in a cloud of glory for weeks afterward.

Summer Sees What Jesus is Like from Eddy

I remember thinking, if that is what Jesus is like, like Eddy. He is better than I had imagined. I could see why crowds would follow Jesus to receive the touch they needed from heaven if it was anything like going to a meeting with Eddy. Eddy didn't close the meeting until he had prayed for every person there! No wonder his meetings lasted deep into the night. And every person seemed to leave with a special touch from God.

Of course, that is what Jesus is like. Eddy had become like Jesus by walking closely with Him. What was so exciting to me was seeing someone so much like Jesus. I got to see Jesus' love in action through Eddy. I got to see that those I thought were unlovable were no less important than those I thought of as important. I saw more power coming from a quiet unassuming person than I had ever witnessed in my life. That power was the power of love, God's love. I couldn't wait for Eddy to come back; he said he would be back the next year, but he never returned because he passed away shortly after that meeting.

I learned about Jesus from Eddy Walker. I learned what Jesus' love looks like. Each person that stood before Eddy was, in that moment, the most important person in the world to him. Jesus is like that. It wasn't that Eddy was so dynamic; he was quite a humble little fellow. It was that he, through a close walk with the Lord, was mirroring Jesus. This was lacking in my life. I didn't see everyone as important. I was young and very immature, and I judged people's worth much as the world does. I didn't even measure up in the standards I thought were important. I was beginning to now. I was kind of like the Pharisees in Jesus time, thinking God shouldn't bother with some people. To the Pharisees it was the sinners who they felt didn't deserve Jesus' attention, to me it was the old fat church ladies that would moan and cry through all the meetings. {Now, 37 years later, I am an old fat church lady who moans and cries through every church service.}

The love of Jesus, in this little old man made him the most desirable person I had ever seen in my life. I wanted to be just like him, because in him I saw Jesus.

Jesus' Amazing Walk of Love

When Jesus walked the earth He walked in love. He lived love. He valued people, all people. He healed the lepers, the absolute cast-offs of society. No one in that time would even go near them. He talked to the woman at the well. Not only was she a sinful woman, but she was also a woman. In that day, they were considered inferior. Also she was a Samaritan. All three were taboo, did Jesus care? No!

And He held and blessed the children. When the disciples tried to shoo away the children, Jesus wouldn't let them. He saw them as important, very important. His disciples thought they were a nuisance.

Then He healed the servant of a Roman soldier, the enemies of the Jews. The Jews hated the Romans and were looking for a leader to free them from their influence. In fact, they thought Jesus was that leader. But Jesus was amazed at the faith of the centurion, and He healed his servant. He valued Romans as well.

Not only did Jesus live the love He had for people in His actions and His words. His teachings taught us to love others also. He taught us something totally revolutionary to our human way of thinking. *"You have heard that it was said, 'You shall love your neighbor and hate your enemy.' But I say to you, love your enemies, bless those who curse you, do good to those who hate you, and pray for those who spitefully use you and persecute you, that you may be sons of your Father in heaven; for He makes His sun rise on the evil and the good, and sends His rain on the just and the unjust." Matthew 5: 43-45*

Jesus taught us to love our enemies. To love those, we would normally hate. Everything around us teaches us different. We value looks, brains, talent and youth. We value fame, wealth and position. When we have these things, we soar with pride and look down on those who don't. If we don't have these things, we desperately long for them or try to hold onto them so we can feel some worth in ourselves. Jesus is not like we are, His perspective is different. People hold a higher value to Him than we could possibly imagine.

Our Society Only Values Certain People

I remember when I first moved to Florida. I was not used to seeing the homeless and the bums, the cast-offs of society. They were everywhere down there. One day not long after we moved there, I was driving down the road when I saw a man lying on the sidewalk, unconscious. I quickly pulled over and ran into the nearest building, a doctor's office. "I need to use the phone! "I cried. "There is a man unconscious on the sidewalk!"

The receptionist glanced out the window and said, "That's just a bum."

"The man is unconscious," I repeated. "I need to call for help." The receptionist refused to let me use the phone. This man, who was unconscious in front of the doctor's office, was worthless to them! I couldn't convince anyone in that office to even let me use the phone. I had to drive home and call.

People are expendable in our society, and not just bums. Money is more valued than human life. We see it over and over in our society and not just the bank robber who shoots someone in a hold-up. We see this everywhere. How about the corporations which produce food, with no value to the human body replacing ingredients with harmful substances just for profits? Their profits are more valuable than the health of people.

Or how about abortion clinics, that for profit, will kill a beautiful child? The doctor's that are performing the abortions see first-hand as the baby flinches and fights for life, but the tiny child is defenseless against someone so much larger than themselves. Then this precious human life's body is discarded like common trash. Because they are tiny and unseen, they are considered worthless by many, but not to God. They are an eternal being and although discarded by the world, heaven welcomes them with open arms. They have great value there!

And we have all seen stories on the news about husbands who kill their own wives, rather than split up their belongings in a divorce settlement. The same wife they vowed before God to protect. It is happening in alarming rates. It is over money, worldly wealth, a house a car a bank account, the things that Jesus puts very little value on.

What Makes Us Valuable?

Jesus is not like we are. His perspective is different. He puts a higher value on people than we can possibly imagine. When God paid the ransom for us, for people, He did not use nearly worthless worldly wealth. In fact, there was nothing on earth that He could find that could possibly be worth the value of a human being to Him. He had to look in heaven and He chose the most valuable thing to Him, His Son. God redeemed us with the blood of His Son. All of the Godhead, Father, Son and Holy Spirit were represented in that shed blood.

So deep is the love of God for mankind. The value God places on each one of us is unbelievable. It is because of the greatness of His love for us that He paid such a huge price for us, each of us, and that is what makes us valuable! Because the greatness of our Creators love for us. From the bum on the street to the unborn child to the inmates in a prison, they are all of incredible worth, because God values people!

If you were to handle something of value for a friend, say it was a vase, a Ming vase. And you found out this friend paid millions of dollars for this vase. Would you handle it with care? Yes, you would because of the huge price and value they placed on the vase. God's love for us and the huge expense He had to pay for us makes us priceless. Handle people with care. God released this power of love and this value, toward us as He sacrificed Himself for us. His love for us is a mystery that we will never understand in this lifetime.

The angels who see God, were astounded at this. They could not believe it and wondered why God would give such attention to fallen man! But the angels consider it a high honor and privilege to come to earth and serve fallen man because of the esteem God pays us.

Some people do not even value themselves and I was one of them. I felt I had no worth at all, and I treated myself accordingly. Anyone could do anything to me, and it didn't matter. I gained self-worth from a personal encounter with Jesus. He told me He loved me. He came down from heaven on September 1, 1975, came into the room I was in and told me He loved me. Suddenly I realized I was worth something to somebody and that somebody was Jesus. I stopped abusing myself with cigarettes, alcohol, drugs and inhalants. Jesus became and still is the most important thing in the world to me because my value came from Him.

That Christ may dwell in your hearts through faith; that you being rooted and grounded in love, may be able to comprehend with all the saints what is the width and length and depth and height- to know the love of Christ which passes knowledge; that you might be filled with all the fullness of God.   Ephesians 17-19

Jesus' love passes knowledge. We can begin to follow our example, Jesus, by walking in love. It is a supernatural walk. The first step to walking like Jesus is to value people, His creation. In fact, Jesus told us *"You shall love the Lord your God with all your heart with all your soul and with all your mind. This is the first and greatest commandment. And the second is like it: You shall love your neighbor as yourself." Matthew 22:37*

Jesus Values All People

Jesus valued and loved people. He did not love and value things, or money, or comfort, He loves people and that includes you. His value of you is not dependent on what you look like. You can be ugly it does not affect your value. Or His value on you is not affected by how much money you have, your age, your weight, how smart you are, how much you have sinned, etc. etc. etc..

As we begin to follow our example, Jesus, we are going to have to value what He values, PEOPLE! We need to value all kinds of people, every kind of people, even ourselves. This was new to me. And I have had to learn this lesson again and again. Now, Jesus' words will start to make sense to us. Now, we can start to understand them.

"But I tell you not to resist an evil person. But whoever slaps you on the right cheek turn the other to him also. If anyone wants to sue you and take away your tunic, let him have your cloak also. And whoever compels you to go one mile go with him two. Give to him who asks you, and from him who wants to borrow do not turn away. Matthew 5:39-42

Jesus tells us to love our enemies, to do good to those who hate us. Jesus our example is teaching us to value people. Jesus even values evil people. Are you seeing that if you were to hold people as the most valuable things on earth, you will finally understand what Jesus your example is all about? And then you will change the way you live, if people become more valuable to you than things. When you begin to see all people as valuable, even the deepest sinner, because of the price that Jesus paid for them, because of their worth to Him. Then you will hold all people dear, like He does.

You will begin to understand and do Jesus' teachings, the hard teachings, the ones that never made sense before, like loving your enemies and turning the other cheek, and giving more to those who sue you. Are you beginning to see that all people have value, not just desirable people?

I never knew how much like Jesus someone on earth could become until I met Eddy Walker. Eddy learned to walk in love. He thought of each person as a present from God to him. He wouldn't close a meeting until he had prayed for each one there. He had learned to value people as Jesus did. He learned to walk in love as Jesus did because he was following the greatest example of love, our example JESUS!

Chapter Two

Jesus Walked in Humility

Let this mind be in you which also was in Christ Jesus. Who, being in the form of God, did not consider it robbery to be equal with God, but made Himself of no reputation taking the form of a servant, and coming in the likeness of men. And being found in appearance as a man, He humbled Himself and became obedient to the point of death, even death of the cross. Philippians 2:5-8

Jesus walked in humility in His life on earth. The creator of the universe, the One that sits on the highest throne at the right hand of God. The One of whom every knee in heaven and earth will bow, our Jesus, lived a humble life. He was born in a barn and laid in a manger, a humble beginning. He was most likely a carpenter until He began His ministry. And before Jesus ministry began, we know very little about Him. He seemed to lay low until God's appointed time. He did not promote Himself. He did nothing for personal gain. He lived and died on this earth in a humble way.

He submitted Himself to God's will. He laid down His life. He did not fight back when He was beaten in fact,

He did not even utter a word. He did not threaten, He did not resist. He could have stopped His crucifixion at any moment. After all, He had the power to stop storms, walk on water, raise the dead. But He only used this power in obedience to the Father. Even though He was God, He did not need to prove it. He stayed on the cross. He walked in humility! He is our example.

Pride the Opposite of Humility

The Bible has a lot to say on humility. The Bible also has a lot to say on pride, the opposite of humility. Satan's sin was pride. Satan and how he operates, and how the world operates, is the total opposite of humility. Satan demands worship. He seeks to promote himself. When his plans are frustrated, he always seeks revenge. Pride is how Satan fell. We learn about it in *Isaiah 14:12-15 How you are fallen from heaven, O Lucifer, son of the morning! How you are cut down to the ground. You who weakened the nations! For you have said in your heart: ' I will ascend in to heaven, I will exalt my throne above the stars of God; I will also sit on the mount of the congregation on the farthest sides of the north; I will ascend above the heights of the clouds, I will be like the Most High.' Yet you shall be brought down to Sheol, to the lowest depths of the pit.* Satan's sin was pride. And his pride caused him a fall. He was kicked out of heaven.

Evil has originated with pride. We need to get rid of pride. The way of humility protects us from pride. Pride will bring us down. It brought Satan down.

Pride Always Brings Us Down, Humility Always Brings Us Up

I am going to make a powerful statement I want you to remember. If you get nothing else from this chapter get this. Pride will always bring you down and humility will always bring you up. Pride comes before a fall; humility comes before promotion. God hates pride, He resists the proud. God loves the humble; He hears them when they call on Him. Remember, humility up, pride down. Now I am going to give you some scriptures that say the exact same thing.

Therefore, He say says: 'God resists the proud but gives grace to the humble.' Therefore, submit to God resist the devil and he will flee from you. Humble yourself in the sight of the Lord and He will lift you up. James 4:6-7 and 10.

The fear of the Lord is the instruction of wisdom, and before honor is humility. Proverbs 15:33

"But he who is greatest among you shall be your servant. And whoever exalts himself will be abased, and he who humbles himself will be exalted." Matthew 23: 11-12

Pride goes before destruction and a haughty spirit before a fall. Better to be of a humble spirit with the lowly, than to divide the spoil with the proud Proverbs 16:18-19

By humility and the fear of the Lord are riches honor and life. Proverbs 22:4

For thus says the High and Lofty One, Who inhabits eternity, Whose name is Holy; "I dwell in the high and holy place, with him who has a contrite and humble spirit, to revive the spirit of the humble and to revive the heart of the contrite ones." Isaiah 57:15

Are you beginning to see the value of humility? True humility is not weakness. It is strength. It is obedience and submission to God through the authority that He has placed over you. It is not easy to do. It is a respect for God and for others. True humility is not being wimpy. Humility is pleasing to God, who sees everything. It is not promoting yourself because you think you know it all, or that you are better than someone else. It is completely the opposite of pride.

Humility is also agreeing with the truth. It admits the truth about oneself whether good or bad. Whereas pride lifts itself up and as in Satan's case, over God!

Jesus Teaches Humility to His Disciples

Jesus understood humility and He taught it to His disciples. His disciples thought like the rest of the world thinks and they argued amongst themselves who would be the greatest.

At that time the disciples came to Jesus saying, "Who then is greatest in the kingdom of heaven?" And Jesus called a little child to Him, set him in the midst of then and said, "Assuredly I say to you unless you are converted and become as little children, you will by no means enter the kingdom of heaven. Therefore, whoever humbles himself as this little child, is the greatest in the kingdom of heaven. And whoever receives one little child like this in my name, receives Me." Matthew 18:1-5

This is so opposite to our way of thinking; we want

27

to be great. But Jesus is teaching us the way to be great is through humility! The disciples didn't get it because two chapters later in Matthew 20, He has to tell them again.

And Jesus called them to Himself and said, "You know that the rulers of the Gentiles lord it over them, and those who are great exercise authority over them. Yet it shall not be so among you; but whoever desires to become great among you, let Him be your servant. And whoever desires to be first among you, let him be your slave- just as the Son of man did not come to be served, but to serve and to give his life a ransom for many." Matthew 20:25-28

As we truly follow our example, Jesus, we will learn to be humble. Jesus came to serve not to be served. Those who follow Him have a servant's attitude. This is good because God loves humility; this is learning to be pleasing to God. He exalts those who walk humbly. A humble person is submissive to authority. A humble person does not promote themselves. A humble person doesn't seek revenge but leaves that to God. A humble person most of all, obeys God. A humble person is a servant.

"If You Hold Your Peace I Will Always Fight for You"

I saw an episode on humility on a Christian television program called *It's Supernatural*. A man named David Jones was the special guest. He had a terrible problem with pride and rebellion. He had a father that would beat him as a child and because of it he developed a very defiant attitude. His attitude was that "no one will hurt me ever again". He hated authority. Because of this he was always getting into trouble. David became a Christian and the Lord began to deal with his prideful, rebellious, attitude, but still it was hard for David.

One day, at David's construction job, David and a coworker almost got onto a fight. The coworker was bossing David around, telling him what to do, and David didn't like it. That prideful attitude kicked in; he didn't let people boss him around. He got angry and picked up a wrench to hit him, but the boss came and broke up the fight.

While David was on break the Lord dealt with him to change his attitude. David repented and began to pray for his coworker, his enemy. The boss tried to keep the two separated from that time on, but the coworker came looking for David. He wanted to fight. David had changed his attitude and refused to fight with him. He acted in true humility. David's humility activated God.

God dealt with his coworker in the night. The next day the coworker came into work with a red swollen face. "Look at me," he said to David. "I woke up this way and it hurts." God had dealt with the man, and he knew it. David prayed for the coworker, and he was healed. From that time on the man treated him with the utmost respect.

The Lord then told him, "David, if you will hold your peace, I will always fight for you."

What a benefit, to have God fight for you! I want to walk humbly. I want God fighting for me!

It Really Works

God wants us to step back and let Him handle bad situations. Our part is to step back. Our humility activates God. I have seen this in my life too. One time, I had a situation like this at work. I work as a home health aide. It was my day off, but my office called me in and asked me to fill in for someone off sick. They sent me to an apartment an elderly woman to give her a shower. I had never met her before. When I arrived, she was upset that her regular girl hadn't come. Her television wasn't working, and she had called a repairman. She wanted a quick shower, in case the repair man came while I was there. She was upset because she thought I would take too long. Everything I did seemed to set her off more. I put the bathmat in the shower, and she hollered, "No it doesn't go in that way!" I turned it the other way. "No not that way either!" I was trying really hard but nothing I did seemed to satisfy her. She kept yelling at me no matter what I did. Finally, about halfway through the shower she started pounding on the side of the tub with her fists and screaming, "Why, why, why, did they send you here today?!!! Why couldn't they send the other girl?!!"

Up until then I had been patient because I realized it was hard on her to have someone new and because it was very important to her to get her television fixed. But when she started pounding on the side of the tub and screaming, I had enough. I was going to tell her that this was supposed to be my day off and I had come in to help her. I opened my mouth to let her have it, but I didn't speak. I changed my mind and kept silent. As she was pounding and yelling, I stood back quietly saying nothing.

The Lord rebuked her. I felt Him in the room, and I saw it on her face. She looked startled and suddenly shut up. She realized she was being ridiculous. She straightened back up and let me give her a shower and never complained again. From that moment on, things went smoothly. By the time I left she was begging me to come again. Just as I was leaving the television repairman arrived. Things went perfectly; God was in control. I was humble and God stood up for me. I was learning this amazing principle about humility.

The Mantle of Humility

I have learned so much about humility from my favorite book, *The Final Quest*. *The Final Quest* is a book about a prophetic vision that the author, Rick Joyner has. I love the parts in the book about humility. They are so powerful. I am going to quote them for you. You need to know some background before I quote the book. In his powerful vision, the author, Rick, and the Christian warriors with him, have just fought a valiant battle with a huge demonic army. They win by fighting from the mountain of the Lord.

The mountain of the Lord has many levels, the first being salvation. Some warriors stay on the lower levels and fight from there. Some climb higher to new levels and continue to fight. Rick is one that climbs. As the Christian warriors climb and fight this evil army, they become more victorious. The glory on their armor and weapons grows brighter and brighter.

At the top of the mountain, they enter the garden of God. There they see the Lord. By the time they enter the garden of God, a place of magnificent glory, they have become great warriors and their armor has become dazzling with God's glory.

Then they come down the mountain after their great victory. As Rick comes down the mountain, he sees the enemy army retreating. He wants to attack what is left of their army when wisdom tells him, "Not yet." Wisdom points over to a valley. Rick tries to see where he is pointing but the glory coming from his armor makes it too hard for him to see. This is when Rick asks wisdom for something to cover his armor so he can see.

I asked Wisdom if there was something that I could cover my armor with so I could see it. He then gave me a very plain mantel to put on. "What is this?" I inquired a little insulted by its drabness. "*Humility,*" said Wisdom. "You will not be *able to see very well without it*." Reluctantly I put it on and immediately I saw many things that I could not see before. I looked toward the valley and the movement I had seen. To my astonishment there was an entire division of the enemy horde that was waiting to ambush anyone who ventured from the mountain.

"What army is that?" I asked, "And how did they escape from the battle intact?"

"*That is pride,*" explained Wisdom. "*That is the hardest enemy to see after you have been in the glory. Those who refuse to put on this cloak will suffer much at this most devious enemy.*"

Our Enemy Pride

I love this vision. It helps me to see how putting on humility increases our vision, our spiritual vision, and protects us against pride that is waiting to attack us, especially after a great victory. The mantle of humility was so plain and ordinary and drab that Rick wasn't very excited about putting it on. But it caused his vision to increase to the point that he could see the enemy's division of pride that was waiting to ambush him. This plain, drab mantle saves him.

This shows us also how much of an enemy pride is. The Lord calls it a most devious enemy that attacks from behind. As the story continues, Rick now sees his companions, the warriors that don't put on the mantle of humility, and how they go out to battle and they are easily defeated and taken captive by the demonic regiment called Pride. They ambush the warriors who advance without humility. He is absolutely dismayed as he watches his companion's defeat. Here is more from the book.

I blurted out. "How could those who were so strong, who have been all the way to the top of the mountain, who have seen the Lord as they have, be so vulnerable?"

"Pride is the hardest enemy to see, and it always sneaks up behind you," **Wisdom lamented.** *"In some ways, those who have been to the greatest heights are in the greatest danger of falling. You must always remember that in this life you can fall at any time from any level."*

"Take heed when you think you stand, lest you

fall," I replied. How awesome these Scriptures seem to me now.

"When you think you are the least vulnerable to falling is in fact when you are the most vulnerable. Most men fall immediately after a great victory," Wisdom lamented.

"How can we keep from being attacked like this?" I asked.

"Stay close to me. Inquire of the Lord before making major decisions and keep that mantle on. Then the enemy will not be able to easily blindside you as he did those."

I looked at my mantle. It looked so plain and insignificant. I felt it made me look more like a homeless person than a warrior. Wisdom responded as if I had been speaking out loud. *"The Lord is closer to the homeless than to kings. You only have true strength to the degree that you walk in the grace of God, and 'He gives His grace to the humble.' No evil can penetrate this mantle, because nothing can overpower His grace. As long as you wear this mantle you are safe from this kind of attack."*

Humility is essential to us. It keeps us from falling. It protects us from pride. It keeps us in God's grace, the safest place to be. Isn't this exciting! It feels so plain and ordinary and drab to Rick, but it protects him from his enemies. Does this remind you of Jesus? The king of heaven walking humbly on earth, this is how He defeated Satan. Jesus clothed Himself in humility. This is the example we are to follow.

I want to quote one more small passage on

humility from the book. This time Rick is in a heavenly place called the Hall of Judgment. It is a huge, glorious hall in heaven. Rick is walking toward the judgment seat of Christ when he notices heavenly hosts on either side of him. They are more glorious than anyone he has ever seen. They are people from earth; they are the cloud of witnesses, the heroes of the faith, those who have gone on before us.

The Highest Rank of Honor in Heaven

Then Rick looks down at himself and sees he has the mantle of humility on. He is embarrassed by his lowly appearance especially around these standing before the throne who were so glorious. He is also afraid to appear before the Lord looking like this. This is when He is told, **"Those who come here wearing that mantle have nothing to fear. That mantle is the highest rank of honor, and it is why they all bowed to you while you passed."**

I quoted that little passage because I wanted you to see that, in heaven, the mantle of humility is the highest rank of honor. Rick is in a heavenly place around the saints who have lived before him. He feels very inferior, cloaked in humility and because of the glorious disposition of these saints. Instead, the saints bow in honor to him. They bow because of the cloak, the mantle of humility. It is such a high honor because it is the mantle that Jesus wore when He walked the earth! When I read that it totally amazed me. It is so opposite of how our world operates. Even in the body of Christ many seek a high position and want to be noticed. But true Christianity, like Jesus lived it, it clothes oneself in humility.

It did not seem desirable to Rick, this mantle of humility, it seemed plain, foul and crude. And yet it caused those in heaven to bow in respect to him. Things will look different to us in eternity than they do to us now. Humility is one of those things. It is the highest rank of honor in that realm.

Benefits of Humility

I have quoted all these passages because of the amazing things I have learned about humility in them. I will sum them up.

Humility keeps us from pride. It keeps us from being attacked from behind. It helps us to see our enemy, pride. It keeps us in the grace of God, the only true strength we can have. Jesus wore the mantle of humility when He walked this earth. We need to put on this mantle just as our example did.

Jesus is our example. He walked the earth in humility. He was not proud or haughty. He did not get puffed up after a great miracle. He did not charge people money. He came as a servant, He served people. But most of all He obeyed God. He laid down His life.

We can do this too. We can put on the mantle of humility. We can walk on this earth as Jesus walked. We can follow His example. We can live a life in obedience to God. We don't have to promote ourselves. We can be humble. We can be submissive to the authority He puts over us and be obedient. We don't need to get even with people or threaten. We can commit ourselves to God like He did. We can keep our mouths shut and God will move for us. We can wear the mantle of the highest rank in heaven, the one Jesus wore, HUMILITY!

{Remember, pride always comes before a fall and humility always comes before promotion!}

Chapter Two

Part B

A Deeper Look at Humility

We just talked about humility. It is amazing stuff, humility. But I want to start all over and look at humility all over again, but this time let's go deeper. Let's dive straight down into the deepness of humility, the humility of our incredible God and get a peek at something so awe inspiring to me and so holy that it takes my breath away.

Humility can seem like a brown paper bag, so ordinary, so lowly. Yet in it is a secret, the secret so big and so beautiful my mind cannot even contain it. I can only try to pull back the veil of eternal things, with mere human words, and try to give you a small glimpse of something that I have only a small glimpse of myself, very small. Let's take a peek together. Let's look at our verse again.

Let this mind be in you which was also in Christ Jesus, who, being in the form of God, did not consider equality with God something to be grasped, but emptied Himself by taking the form of a servant, and coming in the likeness of men. And being found in the appearance as a man, He humbled Himself and became obedient to the point of death, even the death of the cross. Therefore, God has highly exalted Him and given him the name which is above every name, that at the name of Jesus every knee should bow, of those in heaven, and of those on the earth and those under the earth, and that every tongue confess that Jesus Christ is Lord to the glory of the Father. Philippians 2:5-11

We are getting into some very eternal stuff here. We are getting into the relationship between God the Father and Jesus. We know that everything that is, has been created, except, God the Father and God the Son and God the Holy Spirit, they are eternal, they are God, they are three but one. This is something very hard to understand. Back before anything else existed, we have these three. What did they do without us?

God the Father is Love. We are told that God is Love. Love cannot be commanded; love is something that can only be given by choice. Somewhere back before we existed God the Father poured out all His love, on Jesus, and on the Holy Spirit, that is His nature to love. We are told in our scripture Jesus had equality with God. What did Jesus do with His equality with God, with God's love bestowed upon Him! He out of love for the Father emptied Himself. Equality with God belonged to Jesus, it was His, given by love, to do with as He pleased and yet He, in love for the Father, chose to empty Himself, as an act of love and utter humility, and take the form of the Father and become the Son. The exact image of the Father. God gives His all to the Son, in love to do with as He pleases but Jesus chooses to empty Himself and mirror the Father. This is Divine humility, an act of returning the Father's love to Him. We get a little glimpse of this from scripture. Here are some verses.

Most assuredly the Son can do nothing of Himself, but whatever He sees the Father do, for whatever He does the Son also does in like manner. John 5:19

I can of Myself do nothing As I hear I judge; and My judgment is righteous, because I do not seek My own will but the will of My Father who sent me. John 5:30

Philip said to Him, "Lord show us the Father and it is sufficient for us." Jesus said to him, "Have I been with you so long and yet you have not known Me, Philip? He who has seen Me has seen the Father; so how can you say, 'Show us the Father?' Do you not believe that I am in the Father and the Father is in Me?

Jesus has chosen to empty Himself of His own will and identity, which is only known by the Father. Now He submits His identity to the Father, creating a circle of love between Himself and the Father. This is the ultimate in humility and love.

But what about the Holy Spirit? He also has acted in divine humility and emptied Himself even further. He has become nameless and faceless! He is invisible! Jesus speaks of Him in John 16: 13-15 *"However, when He the Spirit of Truth, has come, He will guide you into all truth; for He will not speak on His own authority, but whatever*

He hears He will speak; and He will tell you things to come.
He will glorify Me, for He will take of what is Mine and
declare it to you. All things that the Father has are Mine.
Therefore, I said that He will take of what is Mine and
declare it to you."

This totally blows my mind!!!!! This is powerful stuff. The Holy Spirit is the power behind the universe, and He has totally humbled Himself. He comes to us gently as a still small voice, that is so faint we only hear Him if we choose His voice over the louder voices in our minds. He like Jesus, also, had emptied Himself of self-expression and seeks to glorify Jesus. We have a God which operates together in love and humility with each other, unbelievable love and unbelievable humility. It is a circle of love.

God the Supreme Being of the universe humbles Himself. God the Father has emptied Himself and given Himself to Jesus and the Holy Spirit who have responded in love and emptied themselves of all self-expression in deep humility and come back to the Father and become One with the Father, so we have God acting in One, in love, as One, the Father being the Head. But the circle of love just keeps growing. This doesn't make God smaller it makes Him bigger. Like a nuclear explosion. We split an atom, a tiny particle, but the results are huge! And it multiplies until it explodes with unbelievable power. God's humility causes a reaction, love keeps growing, and the Father gives again. The Father keeps giving now He puts all things under Christ's feet! He makes the name of Jesus above every name. And the Father and Jesus jealously guard the Holy Spirit; we are told that to blaspheme Him will never be forgiven, not only in this age but also the one to come! {Mark 3:28}

We have a circle of love between God the Father, Jesus and the Holy Spirit, that acts in total humility, which keeps expanding. We serve a God who acts in humility that is fueled by love!!!! They act as One and are in perfect unity because of their humility!!!!!

So that is what they were doing before us! But there is something even more amazing!!!!!!!!!! Can you guess what it is?

You can join this circle of ever-growing love! We can become a part of this! Paul writes about it.

I have been crucified with Christ; it is no longer I who live, but Christ lives in me; and the life that I live in the flesh I live by faith in the Son of God, who loved me and gave Himself for me. Galatians 2:20

We can follow the example of the humility of Jesus and empty ourselves and through humility come into God's circle of love and come into perfect unity with the Father and the Holy Spirit through Jesus, in love and humility!

" At that day you will know that I am in my Father, and you in Me and I in you." John 15:20

What an honor! It blows my mind. This is where following the example of Jesus humility, will lead us, to the very heart of God.

Chapter Three

Jesus Came to Serve

And He said to them, "The kings of the Gentiles exercise lordship over them, and those who exercise authority over them are called benefactors. But not so among you, on the contrary, he who is the greatest among you, let him be as the younger, and he who governs as he who serves. For who is greater he who sits at the table or he who serves? Is it not he who sits at the table? Yet I am One among you as one who serves. Luke 22:25-27

Jesus came not to be served but to serve. This goes hand in hand with humility. This is also hard for our minds to grasp. Jesus is the King of all Kings and the Lord of all Lords, the ultimate authority in the entire universe to whom every knee will bow, and yet, He has come to serve. He is so majestic and so glorious that if we were to see

Him in His eternal form, we would not be able to stand before Him but would immediately fall on our faces in awe and wonder, completely overcome by the glory that proceeds from Him. Yet, He came to serve us. We don't even realize the meaning of this.

Jesus is Highly Worshipped in Heaven

Even the angels, His servants, when they appear, have caused humans to fall before them in worship; they have to tell people not to do that. But, the angels, who are glorious and majestic, they worship God and fall before Him. They see the presence of Jesus and are struck with awe at His glory. Can you imagine how we would feel in His presence if the angels who are used to His glory are so overcome by Him. The angels in His presence continually cry out, "Holy, holy, holy!" He is revered, He is holy, and He is the King. And yet, He came to earth to serve.

In our realm, we don't understand the significance and the power of Jesus the Son of God. We don't understand the awe and respect that is paid to the King of all Kings, our Creator, our Redeemer, our Lord. It is hidden in our reality. Some even use His name as a swear word. Unlike the angels we don't know Him as He is, because He came in the form of a servant.

Roland Buck in his wonderful book, *Angels on Assignment,* has described the angel's reaction when Jesus briefly appeared. This is a wonderful book about a man who is visited by angels. He is speaking with an angel in this passage that I will quote for you.

He told me about different angels, such as praise angels, worship angels, ministering angels and warrior angels. Regardless of their function, their highest purpose is to exalt the name of Jesus! When that name sounds in heaven, or here on earth, they fall face down and worship Him because He is so exalted!

One night while Gabriel and Chrioni were talking to me, there suddenly appeared a bluish shaft of pure light about eighteen inches in diameter from the ceiling to the floor of our study room. The instant the light appeared, both angels fell prostrate on the floor. They stayed in a prone position for at least five minutes without a single motion or sound. I didn't know what to do so I fell on my knees and worshipped God.

Do you see the level of respect the angels pay to Jesus, to His brief appearance or the mention of His name? They fall prostrate and don't move. They don't live in a realm where God's glory is veiled. They understand who He is, and they fall prostrate. This God, this King, Jesus, He came not to be served but to serve.

I often talk about the day I got saved when Jesus walked through the door of my sister's bedroom and spoke to me. Jesus presence had a feeling. The feeling was pure majesty. It had a feeling of Him being the King of Kings and Lord of Lords. The power in the room radiating from Him was unlike anything I had ever felt before. One meeting with His presence had the power to change me forever. I went from darkness to light in that instance. I went from constant turmoil to peace, from death to life. From being a kid, whose parents were at their wits end to one they hardly recognized.

Years later, I felt that feeling again. I was in a church service that met in a rented hall. The pastor was closing the service and asked the elders, there were several, to go stand at the back and pray for people. As the elders and their wives positioned themselves along the back of the room, I felt Him. I didn't see Him, but I sensed Him, and I knew exactly where He was. I knew it was Jesus because I had the feeling of royalty again. I don't know how else to describe it, it was powerful. The whole room felt electric. The room came alive. I felt the hair on the back of my neck stand up and I felt breathless. I don't know if anyone else there sensed Him, but I did. I knew exactly where He was. He walked through the wall and went and stood next to a particular elder and His wife.

I watched that corner of the room; I knew something was going to happen. The person who went back there for prayer had a divine appointment with God that day. It was a lady and as she got prayed for, I heard her shriek and then she fell to the floor, slain in the spirit.

Jesus presence is pure majesty.

I have a book called, *The Archko Volume*. The book is amazing. It contains ancient writings that come from the Vatican in Rome, records from the time of Jesus. In the 1850's a man named W.D. Mahan found out about these records and went to great lengths to get a copy. They were copied by a monk who had access to them, and then translated and sent to him. One of the writings is a record from Pilate and he records a meeting he had with Jesus. I am not going to go into what was said between them, but I just want to write the feelings Pilate describes when he met Jesus, I think Pilate felt what I felt in Jesus' presence.

I wrote to Jesus requesting an interview with him at the praetorium. He came. You know that in my veins flows the Spanish mixed with Roman blood—as incapable of fear as it is of weak emotion. When the Nazarene made his appearance, I was walking in my basilica, and my feet seemed fastened with an iron hand to the pavement, and I trembled in every limb as does a guilty culprit, though the Nazarene was as calm as innocence itself. When he came up to me and stopped, and by a signal sign he seemed to say to me, 'I am here,' though he spoke not a word. For some time, I contemplated with admiration and awe this extraordinary type of man—a type of man unknown to our numerous painters, who have given form and figure to all the gods and heroes. There was nothing about him that was repelling in its character, yet I felt too awed and tremulous to approach him.

Pilate felt it too, and he was some sort of royalty, but he was standing before the King of all Kings.

He is highly exalted in Heaven, yet He came to earth in the form of a lowly servant. That awesome presence put on flesh and came to earth in a humble way. To truly follow Jesus' example, we must do this also, we must become a servant and seek to serve.

The Difference Between Kingdoms

This is the attitude of heaven, but not of earth. On earth, where the kingdom of Satan and the kingdom of God come into conflict, we don't see this attitude of a servant much. Satan and his followers seek to dominate. They seek to be served and seek control over others. His system oppresses the weak and uses them without mercy. Satan and his followers' lust for power and see service as weakness.

But we have been set free from his kingdom and now we belong to the kingdom of heaven. The citizens of heaven are servants. They follow their example Jesus, they live to serve, they serve out of love, and they have regard for the weak.

I love to read testimonies of people who have visited heaven. I have read as many as I can find, and I have noticed something about heaven and the inhabitants that live there. It is the reason why heaven is such a wonderful place. They seek to serve. It is the citizens of heaven's joy to serve others. Those we see as the heroes of the Bible, the patriarchs, those we love to read about, they are happily serving in heaven it is their joy to do so. Those who visit heaven tell of being guided on tours by Moses and Jonah, King David and always they see Abraham. Abraham's place is in Paradise, the outskirts of heaven. This is where he greets the new arrivals and welcomes them home. He is holding a golden goblet that he dips in the river of life and gives a drink to those new to heaven. He is serving the newcomers! Can you imagine living in an atmosphere where everyone seeks to serve?

Jesse Duplantis, in his book of his trip to heaven called, *Heaven Close Encounters of the God Kind,* was escorted through heaven by King David. I'll quote you this portion.

Jesus put his arm around me as He watched a man

walking toward us who was wearing a crown. Then He said to me, "I want you to meet another king."

I recognized him as the man I had seen earlier. He had reddish hair and a red beard. I knew immediately it was David. As he approached us, he spoke to Jesus, "To the great King of kings I bow."

Jesus said, "Jesse, I want you to meet the king of Israel." The Lord said, "Take Jesse to his home. Show him what I have prepared for him. Then bring him to the throne. I must go. My Father wants Me." Then He turned and walked off.

I looked at the man Jesus had introduced and said; "Hello" I didn't know what else to say. "Your name is David, isn't it?"

He answered, "Yes."

Bowing down I said, "Oh king!"

"Don't bow to me." he said. "You've just looked at the King of kings. I've been assigned to take you around."

I asked, "Is there anything I can do for you?"

He replied, "You don't understand; we're servants here. We're here to serve you. What do you want Jesse? What do you need?"

I love that passage. It blows my mind. A king asked Jesse, what does he want and what does he need. The king acts as a servant. We are citizens of this wonderful place. We need to begin to act like they do. We need to begin to serve.

How Do We Serve?

How can we begin to serve? Is there someone who

has a need that you can fill? You can begin in your own home and move on from there.

Wives, does your husband feel discouraged? Can you serve him with your words and attitude? Can you build his self-esteem and lift his load?

Husband, is your wife bogged down with a full-time job and home? Can you take a turn with dishes, laundry and the vacuum?

Can we move on from there? Is there a need we can fill? Do you have something someone needs? Do you have a crib in the attic that young new mother might need or an extra coat that homeless man could wear?

Can you drive someone to work with you who doesn't have a car? Can you invite over someone who is lonely? Is there an elderly person who needs something from the store or a ride to church? A child in your sphere of influence, who has no one to mentor them?

Look around, do you see a need you can fill, a problem you could solve, something you no longer use that you could share? This is where you can begin.

Jesus Washed the Disciples Feet

Jesus knowing that the Father had given all things into His hands, and that He had come from God and was going to God, rose from supper and laid aside His garments, took a towel and girded Himself. After that He poured water into a basin and began to wash the disciples' feet, and to wipe them with the towel which He was girded. So, when He had washed their feet, taken His garments and sat down again, He said to them, "Do you know what I have done to you? You call me Teacher and Lord, and you say well, for so I am. If I then your Lord and Teacher, have washed your feet, you also ought to wash one another's feet. For I have given you an example, that you should do as I have done to you." John 13:3-5 and 12-15.

Jesus just before leaving earth gave this example of serving and this command to serve. I think we have lost sight of this command. I think we live much as the world does. We need to remember this commandment. It is interesting how the early church lived.

The Early Church Lived Much Like Heaven

The early church was of one heart and one mind and they served each other. We first hear of this in Acts chapter 2:44-47 *Now all who believed were together, and had all things in common, and sold their possessions and goods, and divided them among all, as anyone had need. So, continuing daily with one accord in the temple, and breaking bread from house to house, they ate their food with gladness and simplicity of heart, praising God and having favor with all people. And the Lord added to the church daily to those who were being saved.*

I find this very amazing, the people on earth living like the people in heaven. They truly lived as servants. I wonder if we, the body of Christ, will ever live on earth like this again. I know I have a long way to go. Being a servant means living for others.

Modern Day Servants

I can think of many modern-day people who have done this, lived the life of a servant. Mother Teresa lived a selfless life on earth and served the dying. Albert Schweitzer who was a medical missionary to Africa and set up a hospital in the jungle was another. And there was Mark Buntain, a missionary to Calcutta who tirelessly worked to serve the poor setting up a hospital and school and helping countless of children and the sick and the poor. And there is one of my all- time favorites Franklin Graham whose ministry Samaritan's Purse seems to circle the entire globe reaching the needs of the hurting everywhere. These are the ones we see but remember God sees every act of kindness and He promises us even a glass of water given in His name will not go unrewarded.

Let us open our eyes and look around. Let us join heaven and serve. Is there a need we can fill? Let us look to our Example, Jesus who didn't come to be served but to serve. Look at those around you, your families and those you come in contact with. How can you serve them? If you do this, you will be following the example of Jesus.

Chapter Four

Jesus Did Not Fear

And do not fear those who kill the body but cannot kill the soul. But rather fear Him who is able to destroy both soul and body in hell. Matthew 10:28

Jesus faced everything without fear. He taught us to fear only one thing and that was to fear God. Jesus' example to us is to face life without fear. How could He do this?

Because of His absolute faith in God.

We people on earth are quite the opposite of Jesus. Most of us have many fears but we lack the one fear we need to have, the fear of God. That is evident in our society. We see it everywhere. Turn on your television set, adultery is glorified. Movies are full of profanity and every sin.

It is also lacking in our government; politicians stand up and tell lies to the whole nation. Our courtrooms are offended by the Ten Commandments. Schools cannot mention God, and colleges teach everything but God. They teach ridiculous theories of a creation that somehow proceeded out of nothing. There is no fear of God. They forget they will stand before God and give account for not only our actions but every word we speak.

"But I say to you that for every idle word men may speak, they will give account of it in the Day of Judgment". Matthew 12: 36 We have everything backwards. Jesus has everything forwards, He is our example. Let us look at how He lived without fear. Let us talk about some of the things Jesus was not afraid of.

Jesus Did Not Fear Lack

Jesus did not fear lack. We see this in His teachings to us. *Therefore, I say to you, do not worry about your life, what you will eat or what you will drink; nor about your body, what you will put on. Is not life more than food and the body more than clothing? Look at the birds of the air, for they neither sow nor reap nor gather into barns; yet your heavenly Father feeds them. Are you not of more value than they? Which of you by worrying can add one cubit to his stature? So why worry about clothing? Consider the lilies of the field, how they grow: they neither toil nor spin; And yet I say to you that even Solomon in all his glory was not arrayed like one of these. Now if God so*

54

clothes the grass of the field, which today is and tomorrow is thrown into the oven, will He not much more clothe you, O you of little faith? Therefore, do not worry, saying, 'What shall we eat?' or 'What shall we drink?' or "What shall we wear?' For after all these things the Gentiles seek. For your heavenly Father knows that you need all these things. But seek first the kingdom of God and His righteousness, and all these things will be added unto you. Matthew 6:28-33

We see in Jesus' life that He did not worry about these things. He never hoarded or stockpiled food. When the multitude was hungry, He told the disciples you feed them. Twice He fed huge masses of people with a small amount of food, a couple of fish and a couple loaves of bread. He certainly did not worry about it.

Then there was the time in Matthew 16:11, when the disciples were concerned because they brought no bread, Jesus had spoken to them of the yeast of the Pharisees. Jesus asked them about how many baskets of food were left after they fed the five thousand and the four thousand; He was not concerned they had brought no bread. He was not worried about food! He was speaking of the false teaching of the Pharisees and was amazed that the disciples thought He was concerned about food. Food was something He knew His heavenly Father would provide!

Jesus is teaching us an amazing principle here. If we seek the Kingdom of Heaven first, then amazing provision comes to us, we don't need to be concerned or seek it, it is there when we need it. Like enough food to feed thousands.

Jesus didn't even worry about his taxes. He sent

Peter out to catch a fish and told him to open the mouth of the first one he caught; in it he would find a coin to pay both their taxes. Peter did it. Jesus walked through this life without the fear that many of us have, the fear of not having enough, He didn't fear lack. What else?

Jesus Did Not Fear Sudden Dangers

We see a perfect example of this in in Mark chapter four, Jesus is sleeping in the bottom of the boat. A great windstorm had arisen, and they were filling up with water. The disciples woke Him up and cried, "Don't you care that we are perishing?"

They were terrified. Jesus stood up and rebuked the wind and the waves. Then He asked them, "Why are you so fearful? How is it that you have no faith?"

Things like huge storms did not scare Him. They did not need to be afraid because Jesus was in the boat! If you are serving Jesus; He is in your boat too! He had authority over things like the wind and the waves. He certainly did not fear drowning; He walked on the water during a storm with large waves!

Jesus Did Not Fear People

Many times Jesus spoke the truth and it did not make Him popular with people. He was never moved by what people thought of Him. There were several times that as He spoke the people became so enraged that they tried to kill Him. In Luke chapter four was one of those times. The people led Him to the top of a cliff to throw Him off. Jesus was not afraid of people's opinions and He did not live His life to please them, He lived to please His Father. He did not have to twist the things He said to avoid offending the popular thinking of the times. Every generation has a current set of untruths they hold to, that is called popular thinking. Popular thinking does not stand the test of time and will change.

Popular Thinking Is Not the Truth

Popular thinking in our country only a short time ago allowed slavery and saw a race of people as inferior. True followers of Jesus did not embrace that thinking and were opposed to it. Even the government, for a while followed the popular thinking and allowed these horrors to continue. Many of those that opposed it had to disobey the laws, they formed underground railroads.

Although in their time they seemed to be the ones who were wrong {the true Christians}, when the smoke of the deception, of the popular thinking of their timed cleared, they became heroes and are remembered that way to this day.

Popular thinking in our time deals with unborn children and sexual deviancies. These are untruths and will not stand the test of time, but currently the Christian view is not popular. Those who oppose these deceptions are facing some of the same challenges others in ages past have faced, when standing for the truth.

Jesus faced popular thinking in His time, women were considered inferior and Samaritans were despised, and the Pharisees did not represent the heart of God they made a pretense of holiness but showed no love and compassion. Jesus' fearless speaking of the truth enraged them and caused them to seek His death.

Another example of this was when the religious leaders decided it was wrong to heal people on the Sabbath. I can't believe how ridiculous that was, but they watched to see if He would do it, and He did. He did not let fear of man hinder Him. He healed on the Sabbath and He rebuked the religious leaders for being hypocrites. They wanted to kill Him because of it. He did not fear man; He feared God.

Jesus Was Not Afraid of the Devil

Jesus had come face to face with the devil. He faced him and boldly resisted him, when Satan tempted Him in the wilderness. Jesus cast out demons continuously. One man had a legion of demons in him. We also know that Jesus entered hell at His death. I'm not sure quite what happened but the earth shook and many of the righteous dead came out of their graves. It was powerful. Jesus came out the winner and Satan came out the loser. Evil can be a frightening thing and it is not pleasant to face, but Jesus fearlessly faced the devil and defeated him. Although He didn't take it lightly, He fasted forty days before He faced Satan.

Jesus Was Not Afraid of His Enemies

Jesus' enemies had come to try trip Him up with

hard questions. We see this in Matthew 22; they sent different people to ask Him questions to entangle him. They asked him about paying taxes to Caesar. Jesus astounded them with His answer. He asked them to show them the coin to pay the tax. He asked whose picture was on it. They told Him Caesars. Jesus replied, "Render therefore to Caesar the things that are Caesar's and to God the things that are God's." His enemies continued and each time He confounded them until the Bible tells us "No one dared question Him anymore."

Jesus was not afraid when the detachment of troops and officers came to arrest Him. "Whom are you seeking?" He asked them.

"Jesus of Nazareth," they replied.

Jesus said, "I am He." When He spoke, they all fell to the ground. They couldn't stand before Him, and yet He submitted Himself to them. He faced them bravely. Jesus was tortured. He was at the hands of evil ruthless men. They mocked Him and spit on Him. They stripped Him, beat him and pressed thorns into His head, they pulled out His beard. He did not utter a word. He was not afraid of them, and He told us not to fear those who can only kill our bodies. He is our example.

Jesus Did Not Fear Death

Jesus did not fear death; He called it going to the Father. He taught us this. In Him we have nothing to fear when facing death, because He went before us and made a way defeating death. *"Death is swallowed up in victory. O death where is your sting? O hades where is your victory?" 1Corinthians 15:54b-55* Again He is our example!

Why Jesus Wasn't Afraid

Jesus came to earth as a man. He did this to redeem us. He had to come to earth through natural means and save us in a legal way. He didn't beam down in a ray of light. He was born a baby and had to grow up just like we do. He did everything by faith, just as we have to. He faced the same challenges we face. He walked ahead of us in a human way so that we could follow Him, but His walk on earth was perfect. But He said that we could do greater works than He did.   {John 14:12}

Don't think because He was God that it is impossible to live as He did, because He is our goal, our example. He lived without fear to show us we can live without fear. Jesus lived without fear because He lived in faith, because he trusted God, and because He lived in the fear of the Lord as we should. The fear of the Lord is the good kind of fear.

The Fear of the Lord Versus the Fear of Man

We are seeing that most of us on earth have things backwards we are not afraid of what we should be {God} and we live in fear of what we shouldn't. Most of us have many fears, some of us irrational uncontrollable fears, but one of the biggest fears that hold us back is the fear of man.

We care too much what people think. We care more what people think than what God thinks. Or we are afraid of what men can do to us. We are afraid at work that we will lose our job and lose everything. We are afraid to tell people the truth about God because it is not acceptable conversation. We are afraid to stand up for what is right, because popular thinking is opposite of the truth. We live in fear.

The Bible tells us, *The fear of man brings a snare, But whoever trusts in the Lord shall be safe. Proverbs 29:25*

"Listen to Me, you who know righteousness, You people in whose heart is my law: Do not fear the reproach of men, Nor be afraid of their reviling's. For the moth will eat them up like a garment, and the worm will eat them like wool; But my righteousness will be forever, And My salvation from generation to generation." Isaiah 51:7-8

Jesus did not fear man, we see that in everything He did. He spoke the truth even when it seemed strange, or even when it angered those around Him. He obeyed God no matter how much the people around Him tried to intimidate Him. He had the good kind of fear, the fear of God.

The fear of the Lord is the beginning of wisdom; A good understanding have all those who do His commandments. Psalms 111:10

Surely, His salvation is near to those who fear Him Psalms 85:9

Oh how great is Your goodness. Which You have laid up for those who fear You, Which You have prepared for those who trust in You in the presence of the sons of men! Psalms 31:19

The secret of the Lord is with those who fear Him, and he will show them His covenant. Psalms 25;14

The fear of the Lord is the beginning of knowledge, but fools despise wisdom and instruction. Proverbs 1:7

In the fear of the Lord is strong confidence, and His children will have a place of refuge. Proverbs 14:26

In mercy and truth atonement is provided for iniquity; And by the fear of the Lord, one departs from evil. Proverbs 16:6

The fear of the Lord comes from an eternal perspective. It looks forward to the day we stand before God, and then causes us to live our lives accordingly. The fear of the Lord helps us peek through the heavy veil of darkness that covers our planet, that veils us from the truth of God's eternal omniscient presence and see the real truth so we can live differently.

On the day we stand before Him, we will have no excuses, we can't blame our actions on those around us. We will have to answer for ourselves, and everything will be laid bare.

Jesus had an eternal perspective and that is why He did not fear men but God only.

Summer's Struggles with Fear of Man

The thought of living without fear is so revolutionary to me it is almost unbelievable. I have lived with fear as long as I can remember. God has brought me a long way, in this struggle, but I still have a long way to go.

My whole life I have felt like a leaf blowing in the

wind, I am at the mercy of forces beyond me. One of my biggest fears is of people! It seems they have the power to hurt me; I am at their mercy, so it seems. And there are so many people that have no mercy at all. I am like the can they kick for sport.

Have you ever felt this way? This is called fear of man and since I was a child, I had been consumed with it. I felt the whole world had power over me, and they could hurt me at any time. I especially could not stand any kind of disapproval; this would reduce me to tears at the drop of a hat.

There were different levels of fear I would experience at different times. In places, and with the people I felt safe with, the fear would be a lower level, like a constant stream, but bearable, but still, a cross word could destroy me.

Then there were the harder situations like situations at school or work or even places like court, things you can't get out of, the fear would be all consuming at a roar like Niagara Falls, pounding in my chest and choking me.

Fear of man is a snare; it keeps us from our destiny, and it keeps us from obeying God. I remember one particular time that I disobeyed God because of fear of man. {There were many times.} I had just one child at this time; my little boy was about one year old. My husband worked but we were way behind financially. I had chosen not to work while my children were little because I had suffered abuse from babysitters while I was small.

My mother wanting to help me, found a babysitter for my little boy, a woman who lived in our trailer park, and told me I was coming to work with her the next day. My mother was the supervisor of a kitchen and could do that.

That night the Lord woke me up and told me not to go and not to leave my little boy with the babysitter my mom had lined up. I didn't sleep all that night because I knew I didn't have the courage to tell my mother, no, and that I wouldn't go. I was that afraid of people even my own mother. I always did what people told me to do, I wasn't grown up on the inside, I was a fearful little girl. I told the Lord I couldn't face my mother, so the next day I got up and took my son to the babysitter and went to work.

I felt terrible, but that was normal for me. At about ten thirty my husband called, and he was mad! The babysitter had called him at work to ask him if she could give our son an aspirin because he was crying.

My husband said, "No" and immediately went to check on our son. He said the woman had way too many kids there, the place was a mess and some of the kids were outside without their coats on. He immediately brought our son home and called me angry. "Get home right now and don't ever leave our son there again!"

I felt such relief. Now I had to stay home because my husband gave me no choice. But I wasn't capable of handling things like that, on my own, I had too much fear.

God had to deal with me about fear. He told me things like, this was His world He created it and put me here, I had just as much right to be here as everyone else. He told me when He tells me to do something to do it, and it didn't matter how many people were telling me not to. I was to obey Him! I had to learn to fear Him and do what He says. I began to obey Him. But still my tendency was to stay in my own little corner of the world and not make any waves. I had a little incident that made me realize just how far I had to go.

One day, I had a thought; the thought was, to go see a couple I had worked with when I had delivered newspapers. Their names were Ben and Lois. They were an elderly couple who had lost everything through some poor decisions, and some shady characters. Now they had to work in their old age. They would show up together in an old truck that kept breaking down. After a while it became too much for them and they could no longer keep up.

I hadn't seen them in quite some time. I knew they lived in a trailer home on a small private lot way out of town in the middle of nowhere on a dirt road. I thought it was just a passing thought to go see them. I immediately dismissed the thought because I am not one who likes to get out of her own little world. The thought was like a little fly that flew by and the fear of man in me swatted it immediately, and I never thought about it again.

Sometime later we had a special event at our church. It was a special group to bring in young people and then preach to them and then give an altar call for salvation. They had prayer rooms all set up with counselors to pray with the kids who came to the altar call.

I went and enjoyed the program, and then came the altar call. As they were having the altar call, I had a tug on my heart to go forward.

"I am already saved," I told the Holy Spirit who was tugging at my heart to go forward. The tug grew stronger. I felt silly but I went to the altar. I got herded up with all the tearful young people who were coming to the Lord and sent to the prayer counselors in a side room.

"Do you want to ask Jesus into your heart?" the counselor assigned to me asked.

"I am already a Christian," I told the counselor, "But I felt the Lord tugging on my heart to come forward at the altar call. I am not sure why." The counselor prayed with me that God would reveal to me why I had to go forward for prayer and that was that. I left, somewhat confused.

That night in my sleep, I found out why God sent me forward in the altar call, He was getting my attention. That night, I was not fully awake; I heard God speak to me. He did not speak to me in a still small voice; it was a booming voice, like thunder. I had heard Him in this voice before. I had argued with Him once when He told me to tell someone something. He was using this same voice now; this voice caused every atom in my being to tremble. This voice caused me to FEAR!

"I TOLD YOU TO GO PRAY WITH BEN!" His voice thundered. I then remembered that passing thought I so quickly dismissed. It hadn't even formed into I should pray for Ben but just that I should go there. I wondered how many other thoughts were God trying to speak to me and I just wasn't listening. I was listening to the "fear of man" instead.

"That was you God? I thought that was just a thought in my head."

"GO!"

I had to go, as much as I didn't want to, I was

AFRAID not to. I was more afraid not to go than I was afraid to go, I was afraid of God!

I called Lois and asked if I could come over. I told her I would bring my scissors and cut Ben's hair {I was in beauty school at the time} and that I wanted to pray with him. I thought a free hair cut would get me in the door.

All that week before I went, I was nervous. I kept rehearsing in my mind what to say to lead someone to the Lord. I looked up scriptures, I read gospel tracks. The more I practiced the more nervous I became.

I went to see Ben as scheduled. I could see that his health had declined, and he could no longer hear at all. Lois had communicated to him that I was going to cut his hair and that I was going to pray with him.

I realized how much I loved this precious old man, who had faced much disappointment in his life. As I cut his hair, he held more still for me than anyone whom I had ever cut their hair before or since. He was so respectful.

I could not talk to him because he could not hear me. But after the haircut he knew, I was going to pray for him. He came and sat next to me, and we bowed our heads together. I prayed and asked Jesus to come into his heart. After all my practicing I didn't need to say a word because he couldn't hear me. He just willingly and respectfully bowed before God. God was preparing him to bring him home to Him.

I was so glad this was one-time fear didn't win. I would much rather fear God than men. The rewards are so great. Everything God does is good, even though it seems He stretches us past what we think we can do.

If I live in fear of man, then things are quite

hopeless. If I am at the mercy of people, then they can be incredibly cruel. I would rather live in fear of God, like Jesus did. God has told me to do many things I haven't wanted to do. I didn't think I was capable, but if He tells us to do something then we know that we can do it. I would rather be at the great mercy of God, than that of man. I would rather obey God than my own fears.

Summer Struggles with Fear of Lack

Another one of my big fears has been not having enough. And it was true in my life, we did not have enough. We lived in poverty for many years. God has made progress with me in this area also. I had to learn to obey God, about giving. I would be afraid to obey God in this area. I was afraid God wouldn't provide.

I remember one time when I had to go on welfare. I had been staying in Michigan separated from my husband. I had been so careful to tithe even though I had been on welfare. I had tithed ten percent of my food stamps. I had tithed ten percent of any money I received. After four months my husband came to get me. We had an old station wagon and three kids to drive back from northern Michigan to Florida. Suddenly I realized I hadn't tithed on the rent that the state had paid for me. The amount came to one hundred and twenty dollars. I knew I should pay it, but I was afraid we wouldn't have enough money to get home on. So, I didn't.

Well, we made it home okay but the very next day my brakes went out on my car; it cost exactly one hundred and twenty dollars to fix. I knew this was no coincidence; it was the exact amount I owed in tithes.

God had to do this to me to get me to the point I could obey Him and get blessed. If He told me to give money and I didn't, I noticed something would happen and I would lose that amount any way. I finally wised up, when God would tell me to give money that I felt I couldn't afford, now I gave it anyway, I figured if I don't give what God tells me to I'll lose this money anyway, I might as well obey God and get blessed.

I began to get blessed as I obeyed God. God had to deal firmly with me to help me overcome my fears of lack. Not that I have arrived I am only better than I was. Jesus did not fear lack He did not hoard like I tend to do; He believed God and His needs were met.

Let's Follow Jesus and Live Without Fear

Let's begin to follow Jesus in this area. Let us realize that fear is our enemy and just as Jesus did not let it hinder Him, let us also live for God in this way, free from fear. We will live to please and obey our Heavenly Father. We can do this because Jesus did this and He told us not to fear man who can only harm our physical bodies but to fear God.

I love to just think about it. "I could live without fear." It is a start. I don't have to be afraid of people and I will do what God tells me to do. I don't have to be afraid of disaster, Jesus slept in the boat during a terrible storm that was sinking the ship. I don't have to fear not having enough to eat or drink or wear or a place to live. I don't have to fear the devil or demons; I will resist them like

Jesus did. I don't even have to fear death because Jesus defeated death for me. Jesus lived without fear and so can I, because He is my example.

Chapter Five

Jesus Watched His Words

He committed no sin, Nor was any guile found in His mouth. 1Peter 2:22

Jesus did not sin with His mouth. The word guile means craftiness, cunning, or deceit. The opposite of guile is truth, honesty and sincerity. Jesus could be trusted with his words; therefore, His words were very powerful. He spoke the miracles He performed. He understood words and their power. He commanded the wind and waves to be still. He commanded Lazarus back from the dead. He told the leper to be clean.

The Bible tells us *For we all stumble in many things. If anyone does not stumble in his word, he is a perfect man, able to bridle also the whole body. James 3:2*

Did you catch that? If you do not stumble in your word, you are a perfect man. Jesus was a perfect man, He was our example, He did not stumble with his words.

The book of James is written by James, the earthly brother of Jesus. Think of it, this man grew up living in the same family as Jesus. He saw Jesus in action, in everyday situations. James has much insight into the life of Jesus because he was part of his family. So, what does James write about? He writes about the tongue and learning to control it! He saw firsthand that Jesus controlled His tongue. Jesus never complained, and when He spoke something, He meant it, James saw this and made it an important part of his book.

A Lesson in Watching Our Words

Some time ago my daughter called me early in the morning as I was getting ready for work. She was terrified. "Mom, I have to tell you my dream," she said sounding desperate. "It really wasn't like a dream at all, it was like I was there, like it was really happening, it was so real."

"Well, what was it?" I asked.

"I dreamt David drowned at Twin Lakes."

I gasped. David is her son, my grandson.

There had been several drownings at Twin Lakes in the last few years but even, so it was our favorite place to swim, and we took the kids swimming just about every day in the summer, and this was summer.

"I don't think we better swim there anymore," I told her.

"I don't either," Joy responded.

Joy was still shaken from the reality of dream, so we began to pray fervently in tongues. {This is what we do}

As we prayed, I felt the hair on the back of my neck rise and a feeling of overwhelming evil. Joy felt it too. We prayed harder. Suddenly Joy was silent.

"Mom," she said, "The Lord just told me what this is all about. Remember yesterday."

I did remember yesterday. Joy had lost her temper with David, not that she didn't have her hands full with David. The doctors keep saying he is autistic, but we have refused to accept that. But David can be very hard to handle at times. Joy was so frustrated with David the day before that she had cried out in frustration, "I don't want him anymore!"

I had cringed when she said that. It had upset me.

"Mom, the Lord just showed me when I said that about David yesterday, I opened up a door to Satan, that he could take David's life and that is why I had that dream. It was a warning from God."

I could still feel an evil presence as she spoke; we were having a war with darkness. Joy began to repent for what she said. Not only repent she began to speak life over her son. Finally, our burden lifted. We were grateful for God's mercy that He warned Joy through this dream, but we were both very shaken. But both of us realized that we have got to start watching our words better. This was not funny.

Words Are Spiritual Forces

Why are words so important? Because words are a spiritual force. God created the world with His words. They are how He releases His power. When God speaks something, it has to come to pass. It has to. Once it is spoken it cannot be changed. Can you imagine that? God must be careful with His words because if He says something it becomes so.

Jesus, God in the flesh, carried such power in His word, His words produced miracles on earth, changed weather and He even raised the dead. We are created in God's image. We are meant to have power with our words. What other being can choose their words? Of course, the animals created on earth don't speak. Angels when they speak to us speak to us what God tells them to speak. They bring us a message from God. We are created in God's image and our words contain power. God made us like Himself. We need to realize our words have spiritual power, also.

We Will Give an Account for Our Words

Let us look at some of the things that Jesus taught us about words.

"But let your 'Yes' be 'Yes' and your 'No,' 'No.' For whatever is more than these is from the evil one. Matthew 5:37

We are to be truthful. We are to say only what we mean. If we say we will do something, we have given our word and should do it. We must think before we speak.

"Brood of vipers! How can you being evil, speak good things? For out of the abundance of the heart the mouth speaks. A good man out of the good treasure of his heart brings forth good things, and an evil man out of the evil treasure brings forth evil things. But I say to you but for every idle word men may speak, they will give an account of it in the Day of Judgment. For by your words you will be justified and by your words you will be condemned.
Matthew 12: 34-37

A person's words will show us what is in their hearts. If a person's heart is full of bitterness, it will come out in their speech, if it is full of hatred that will show also. On the other hand, if someone had filled themselves with God's love, you won't hear them cursing or speaking evil.

In conversation with someone, it will not be too long before you know what is in their hearts, good or evil. How about the end of that passage? Every idle word that men speak they will give an account on the Day of Judgment! We need to think about what we are saying! Our words are not just disappearing. They are kept somewhere so we can give an account of them. Let's make it easy on ourselves and use our words wisely.

Words Speak Life or Death to Ourselves

Are you beginning to see how important the words you speak are? Jesus certainly took words seriously. We have been given a great privilege, our words, of which we will have to give an account. Maybe your words are what has been holding you back. Do you say things like

"Nothing I do turns out right."

"I never have enough money."

"I feel a cold coming on."

"I am so depressed."

What are we doing to ourselves? We are cursing ourselves with the power God has given us. Do we do this to others? Yes, we do. Do we want to bring forth good things or evil things to ourselves and to others? I want to bring forth good things!!!! You will not get beyond the words you speak. If you speak poverty, sickness and depression over yourself, you are establishing these things in your life and giving them root. Let's think of our speech as a garden, we want to pull the weeds {negative speech} out of our mouths so the negative things won't take root in our lives. Now we want to speak God's will over ourselves, health, healing, peace, and prosperity and especially praise and thankfulness to God. This puts the fertilizer on the good fruit we want our lives to produce.

The Lord told me one time, "If you don't feel good, don't say it. Even if you are not healed it will pass quicker because it won't have any root."

After He told me that, I tried it. I would feel a cold or sore throat coming on and I would bite my tongue, because I wanted to complain. I noticed that sometimes they would only last a few hours and then they would be gone.

Believe it or not, it is hard work to speak good words. One time, when my son was little, his body became covered with a rash. I kept saying, "It's nothing." Everyone else was upset and telling me to take him to the doctor. It was hard but I just kept saying, "It's nothing." The rash faded by the end of the day, but the other four kids got it, it was the chicken pox and they suffered. I was literally worn out from holding my confession. I didn't have the oomph to do it for the other four kids.

Words Speak Life or Death to Others

Children form their opinion of themselves by the words their parents speak to them. I was in the grocery store one day and heard a mother telling her son what a bad boy he was. I cringed. She is forming that image in the child's mind. That he is bad. We need to speak life to others, especially children!

I know a wonderful Christian man named Jim [my husband]. Growing up his mother told him he was worthless. She found many creative ways to tell him. That was many years ago, and she has passed away, and he told me he still hears her voice in his head saying he is worthless.

Bite your tongue! We need never to do this! If a child does something wrong, we can tell them they did a bad thing! Then we can add that's not like you because you're such a good boy. If a child really is a challenge, we can still strengthen them with our words, and reinforce what God wants to say to the child.

Ephesians 4:29
Let no corrupt word proceed out of your mouth, but what is good for necessary edification that it may impart grace to the hearer.

Satan Wants Your Words

Satan understands the power of words. He wants us to sin with our mouths because it gives him authority over us. If you are a Christian, he cannot operate in your life without your permission. He gets it from your mouth. We need to realize what the devil is after. He wants to trip up your words! It gives him power and authority over you if he can get his negative words to come out of your mouth. Words are spiritual, they affect the spirit realm.

Satan and his demons operate and live on the flood of filth that comes from the mouths of men. Darkness comes out of the mouths of people. I read an example of this in a book by Anna Rountree called, *The Heavens Opened*. Anna is taken by Jesus to a place in Satan's corrupted strata, a place in the second heavens where Satan dwells. She is there with Jesus; she learns much about how evil operates while she is there. The part I will quote you is about words. I will quote her wonderful book.

We came to a levee that sloped down to a black lagoon. The water was filthy, sluggish and stagnant. The smell was putrid. Jesus helped me into a long pirogue. I sat down, but he stood and poled us across the water way with His staff. The water boiled and emitted steam every time His staff plunged into it. Jesus said, "This is a river of filth. As the river of life is clear, so this one is putrid and defiling. It issues from the mouths of sinful man. As rivers of living water come from the belly of my righteous ones, so out of the blackened heart, through

the mouth comes this watery filth."

Our words actually become a substance in the spiritual realm. Ungodly words become a river of filth which Satan uses. This makes me think of movies and television these days. It is like taking a bath in filth. Every foul thing imaginable is said. Satan wants our words for a reason, they empower him.

On the other hand, speaking God's words produces rivers of living water. The author and speaker Kat Kerr mentioned in one of her meetings that she entered a believer's home and saw angels surfing through the house. These people had spoken godly words and had created a river of life running through their home and angels were surfing there. Angels love it when we speak the word of God; it activates them.

This is another situation in which we need to look deeper than what our eyes can see; words matter in the spiritual realm. Your words can give power to the kingdom of darkness, or they can promote life. Many spiritual battles we can win by just holding fast to a confession of faith and not speaking evil over ourselves and others. Profanities have no place on the Christians tongue, neither do idle words. Instead let's speak the word of God and let's speak faith.

Jesus Spoke Faith Filled Words

There were times Jesus spoke in faith. He called things that were not as though they were. When Jesus went to heal Jairius' daughter is such a time.

While He was still speaking, some came from the

ruler of the synagogue's house who said, "Your daughter is dead. Why trouble the teacher any further?" As soon as Jesus heard the word that was spoken, He said to the ruler of the synagogue, "Don't be afraid; only believe." And He permitted no one to follow Him except Peter, James and John the brother of James. Then He came to the house of the ruler of the synagogue and saw a tumult and those who wept and wailed loudly. When He came in, He said to them, "Why make this commotion and weep? The child is not dead but sleeping." And they laughed Him to scorn. But when He had put them all out, He took the father and mother of the child and those who were with Him and entered where the child was lying. Then He took the child by the hand and said to her, "Talitha cumi," which is translated "Little girl I say to you arise." Immediately the girl arose and walked, for she was twelve years of age. And they were overcome with great amazement. Mark 5:35-42

Even though this little girl was already dead Jesus did not say that, He said she was sleeping. He said she was sleeping and then He woke her up. He did not agree with death with His words, He spoke a miracle into existence, and it was so. It did not go over well with the people there. They laughed Him to scorn. {Like I said it is hard work}

Jesus, our example, spoke miracles into existence. He did not even speak what was obviously true, instead He spoke what was about to be true. He did not agree with death. It is okay for us to do this also. We can speak health when we feel sick, we can speak life and light and good over negative situations. We can, Jesus did it. We need to remember not to agree with the negative, even if it appears to be true.

Changing Our Lives with Words

Are there things in your life that need to change?
You will not get past the things you are saying! If you are
speaking poverty over yourself, that is what you will get. If
you are speaking sickness over yourself, you will get that
also. Don't say I can't afford that. Instead, all my needs are
met. My God shall supply all my needs. I hear people speak
all kinds of ungodly things over themselves. No more!
Make your lips a tool to release life, health, prosperity,
encouragement and praise to God. You will become like a
magnet that attracts good things and repels evil.

Fathers and mothers, your words over your children create
their view of themselves. Let them hear you say what a
wonderful child they are. Speak God's blessing on them;
speak that they will serve the Lord all the days of their
lives! Speak love and peace over them.

If God Can Trust You with Your Words, He Will Give Your Words Power

The reason our words don't have as much power as
Jesus words is because God cannot trust us with our
words. When we grow and mature enough that we are
faithful with our words like Jesus was we will be trusted
with more power to our words. Even so our words have
power.

Words Release Faith

"For assuredly, I say unto you, whoever says to this mountain, 'Be removed and cast into the sea,' and does not doubt in his heart, but believes that those things he says will come to pass, he will have whatever he says."
Mark 11:23

I remember hearing Kenneth Hagin speak years ago. Mark 11:23 was his favorite scripture. This scripture raised him from his death bed as a young man and Kenneth preached on this scripture his whole life. What I remember Kenneth saying was the Lord told him that believers were not missing this verse on the believing part, but on the saying part. The word believe is only used once here but the word say is used four times. We need to do four times more saying than believing. Our faith is released through our words.

Satan Had Nothing on Jesus

Jesus on the night of His crucifixion told His disciples Satan had nothing in Him. Jesus had not uttered any careless or evil words; Satan had no authority over Jesus. He had kept His words pure.

I will no longer talk much with you for the ruler of this world is coming, and he has nothing in Me. But that the world may know that I love the Father, and as the Father gave me commandment, so I do. John 14:30-31

Satan gains admittance into people's lives through sin, through deception and through their own words. Jesus lived a perfect life and Satan had nothing in Him. This is the show down, the ruler of this world was coming for Jesus, and all of hell had gathered full force and through mankind were coming for a showdown with the King of heaven.

But Satan has nothing on Jesus, not a sin and not a single word. Jesus willing lays down His life, in obedience to the Father. Seemingly Satan wins the showdown and the king of heaven is abused, tormented, beaten and killed. After death Jesus enters hell. The earth shakes. The sun grows dark. It seems that darkness had won. But darkness hadn't won. Jesus emerges from the grave, carrying the keys to death and hell. He has defeated Satan and all his cohorts. The Bible tells us that He who descended, also ascended, that He might fill all things.

Many times, in our lives it seems that darkness has won. It hasn't. Our victory is In Jesus. We read in Revelation 12:11 *And they overcame him,* {Satan} *by the blood of the Lamb* {Jesus} *and by the word of their testimony, and they did not love their lives to the death.*

This is how we overcome, by the blood of the Lamb and the word of our testimony.

Chapter Six

Jesus Took the Narrow Way

Enter by the narrow gate; for wide is the way and broad is the gate that leads to destruction, and there are many who go in by it. Because narrow is the gate and difficult is the way that leads to life, and there are few who find it.
Matthew 7:13-14

Jesus took the narrow path in His life. Every day He walked the earth He made the decision to stay on the path that led to His death on a cross. It takes singleness of heart and mind to stay on the narrow path. Jesus described the way to life as difficult and narrow.

It certainly was difficult and narrow for Jesus. It took determination and effort, it took courage and selflessness, but Jesus did it. For Him it was the only way! Jesus tells us to count the cost and the cost is everything. Jesus counted the cost, and He went forward, there was no other way. Let's read what He said.

"If anyone comes to Me and does not hate his father and mother, wife and children, brothers and sisters, yes and his own life also, he cannot be My disciple And whoever does not bear his own cross and come after Me cannot be my disciple. For which of you, intending to build a tower, does not sit down and first count the cost, whether he has enough to finish it- lest after he has built the foundation, and is not able to finish it, all who see it begin to mock him, saying ,'this man began to build and was not able to finish.' Or what king going to make war against another king, does not sit down first and consider whether he is able with ten thousand to meet him who comes against him with twenty thousand? Or else, while the other is still a great way off, he sends a delegation and asks for conditions of peace. So likewise, whoever of you does not forsake all that he has cannot be My disciple. Matthew 14:26-33

The Narrow Path Mindset

The cost is great. It was very great for Jesus and it is great for us. The commitment we make to God is greater than any relationship, father, mother, spouse or children, even our own life. The commitment to stay on the narrow path is a commitment to not live for our own pleasure but to follow Jesus where He leads us.

This is the commitment we will need to get on the narrow path in our lives and then, to stay on it! To stay on the narrow path also takes an eternal mindset. We need to live for the world to come, heaven and eternity. This can require sacrificing the things here, that aren't really important there, but seem important here. This is the mindset we need to get on the narrow path and stay there. This is the mindset Jesus had and Jesus was telling us about. We may have to leave love ones behind. We may be misunderstood. We may have to walk alone. It may cost us everything, even our lives. It has many.

The First Fork in the Road

The first fork we come to in life, the one that puts us on the narrow path is our salvation. This is where we begin to follow Jesus. This is where we leave the broad easy path that everyone follows and head a completely different direction.

This truth is so beautifully depicted in the book *Visions Beyond the Veil,* by HA Baker. It is an amazing book about a man and his wife that had a children's home in China, in the 1920's. They took in street children, mostly boys, children ages six to eighteen, and taught them about the Lord. Something amazing happened. These street children of the Adullam Rescue Mission experienced a time of revival, the Holy Spirit was poured out and these unlearned orphans experienced visions of heaven and hell and visions of Jesus coming back. I want to quote you the part about the narrow road, these young Chinese orphans, who were very new to the things of God, saw in their visions.

After the Lord had taken the boys and girls through the most wonderful and systematic lessons in the Holy Spirit, they nearly all came at last to the parting

of the roads. In this vision, repeated until the impression could never be forgotten, the one in the vision seemed to be standing by the cross at the parting of two great roads. The one was the narrow way of life that leads to heaven and glory; the other was the broad way to hell and destruction.

Great, busy, hurrying multitudes- multitudes hustling with business, carrying great loads of sin and rushing along with the affairs of life- were passing in endless streams and countless numbers. The child preacher was at the crossroads. Again, we heard one side of the conversation:

"Hello, my friend! Please wait a minute; I want to speak to you. Say, do not go down that broad road; it leads to hell and ruin. I have been down that way and seen hell for myself. Stop here by the cross and let Jesus wash all your sins away. From the cross of Christ here you can start up this other road that will lead you to heaven and everlasting life and joy. Oh! That fellow does not believe it. There he goes down the broad road. What a pity! I will stop this other man and see if he will believe. Hey there! Just a minute! Say, do not follow that crowd. They do not know where they are going. That road leads to destruction; that road is going to the lake of fire. Please don't go on. I came out here to stop as many of you as possible and give you fair warning. Better turn aside here, let Jesus wash your sins away, and go with us up the road to heaven where God is. Oh, there he goes too!

Here is another. Wait a moment! Say, come out of that crowd. Can't you see there is no one returning? They all go down that road and no one ever comes back. That is the broad road to hell. Stop here by the cross, believe the Gospel of salvation through Jesus' blood, and you'll be safe. There is no other road further on. This is the only road to heaven. Turn in here or you'll be lost too. Oh, what a pity he does not believe me. There he goes on with the others."

Sometimes the youthful preacher would decide that if no one believed him, he would follow the willful crowd to see what happened.

When he arrived with the crowd at the brink of the lake of fire in hell, we heard him say, "Look at the crowd falling into hell! Not one escapes. Everyone goes in."

Slowly drawing near to the edge of the pit and leaning over and looking down into the lake with its suffering multitudes, the preacher said: "I cannot help you now. I told you about this back there at 'The Gospel Crossroads,' but you would not believe. And you still would not believe, even if I could help you out. No, I am helpless now. If you had listened when I warned, the Lord would have saved you; you came on and fell in because you would not take advice. No, I can't. I am going back to the crossroads to see if I can find someone who will listen. I must stop a few at any cost."

He was occasionally successful in persuading one to listen. Then he would say, "Now you get down there at the foot of the Cross of Jesus and pray. Oh, you don't know how to pray? Well you say what I tell you. 'Jesus I am a sinner. I was on my road to hell. I am only fit for hell. The big load I carry is only sin. Forgive my sins and

teach me to live only for your glory. Amen'" There was rejoicing then as the sinner was saved and started up the narrow road, while the preacher went out to try to rescue another deluded traveler.

These Chinese orphans literally saw in their visions the two paths. In an eternal mind set we need to realize that things seen with our spirits are more real than the things we see with our eyes. The spirit world is the real world. There are two paths before us, a broad one and a narrow one. Salvation gets us on the path of life. We continue down it the rest of our lives. These Chinese orphans saw this in the spirit realm firsthand and they saw the destruction where the broad road leads.

More Forks in the Road, The Road gets Narrower

We come to many more forks in the road as we travel the path of life. If we continue to take the narrowest ones, we will continually mature and grow in the Lord faster and it leads to higher callings in Christ.

There are many pitfalls along the way that can slow us down. We can often get off track for a while, we have to repent and make our way back to our wrong turn.

For each person, the path of life may look different. For a young mother it may look so ordinary and plain. It is the path of love and patience, sleepless nights and diapers, bottles and feedings, laundry, meals and dishes. This is the narrow road to life. Know that as you sacrifice each day for your little ones you are taking steps toward the glory of God.

For some the narrow path looks like forgiveness. Some who have traveled this narrow path have forgiven others for unbelievable things such as incest, rape, and even murder. This takes help from Jesus, who from the cross prayed those who were crucifying Him. Those who choose this narrow fork in the road lead themselves and many others, by their example, to freedom.

For some the extremely narrow path looks like bravery. Many on it have risked their lives for others. Some have offered others a body part such as a kidney. Some have laid down their lives on battle fields to save another. Some even lay down their lives, for others or the sake of the gospel. Many of our brothers and sisters in Christ are being martyred for the sake of the gospel. This is an honor that will follow them for eternity.

For some the fork in the road leads to sacrifice. Many have left everything to enter into ministry. They have left good careers, houses and family. Following God's will for their life is more important than anything this world has to offer.

For some, the narrow path means overcoming sins, sins that have been passed down from generation to generation by their forefathers, such as alcohol addiction, incest, lust, adultery and many others. Their narrow path means facing these sins and addictions head on and fighting them until they win. This leads to freedom for future generations that follow them. It takes a huge amount of effort to fight sin, but it is worth it!

The narrow path can seem plain and uninviting to some, it can take tremendous effort for others, but faithfully followed, it leads to joy, peace and eternal rewards.

A Vision of Taking the Highest Mountain to Our Destiny

In an inspiring book called *The Call*, by Rick Joyner, Rick talks of taking the highest mountain, the highest mountain to his destiny. It is the same principle we are talking about with the paths. Rick in this book is in a prophetic vision. He is talking to a young man, named Stephen, who is just beginning his journey out of bondage and to his destiny. The conversation is fascinating. I will quote the book.

I directed him to look at the highest mountain that we could see.

"You must now climb that mountain. When you get to the top, look as far as you can see. Mark well what you see and look for the path that will lead you to where you are going. Make a map of the way in your mind. That is where you are called to go."

"I understand," he replied. "But can it be seen from one of these lower mountains?" I'm no longer afraid of climbing but I am anxious to get on with the journey."

"You can see places from these lower mountains and go to those places much faster. You could choose to do that. It will take longer and be much harder to climb that high mountain, but from there you will be able to see much farther and see something much greater. The journey from the high mountain will be more difficult and take longer. You are free, and you can choose either

journey."

"You always take the highest mountain, don't you?" Stephen asked.

"I know now that it is always the best, but I cannot say that I have always chosen the highest mountain. I have often chosen the easiest quickest way, and I was always sorry when I did. I now believe that it is wisdom to always choose the highest mountain to climb. I know now the greatest treasure is always at the end of the longest, most difficult journey. I think that you, too, are that kind of treasure hunter. You have overcome great fear. Now is the time to walk in great faith."

The path we choose in this life chooses our eternal destiny. The first step is salvation, but the path continues on from there. In this passage we see that choosing the path that takes the most patience and endurance leads to much greater rewards, but the decision is ours. I wanted you to read this passage because it helps us see what we are talking about choosing the narrow path, more clearly. When we choose the higher mountain, or smaller path, we can see farther, we go farther, we learn more patience and we become stronger.

I remember when I first read this passage, I just quoted for you. I don't like difficulties. I put the book down and said to the Lord, "Lord I have never chosen the highest mountain in my life."

"Yes, you have, Summer," the Lord immediately replied, "You chose the narrow path I had for you when you married Jim." I thought about it and realized it was true. Marrying Jim was the hardest and bravest thing I had ever done, and I knew when I married him it was going to be hard; I just didn't know how hard.

I met my husband Jim shortly after he had been paroled for the second time. He had come from a long history of abuse and had been incarcerated almost all of his adult life and much of his childhood.

Jim loved the Lord, and I was the Lord's choice for Jim. I chose a hard path, with God's guidance but God gave me the choice and it was life for me. I wrote that story in my first book *The Impossible Marriage*.

One Woman's Story of Choosing the Narrow Path

I want to tell you another true story of a woman who chose a difficult path for her life, named Ann Sayers. I loved her story so much when I read it because it reminded me of mine. I have treasured this story and read it over and over through the years.

Ann was a single gal in her early thirties. She decided to do some volunteer visiting in a local hospital. While she was there, she met a man named Bill who was in an iron lung. She found out Bill had gotten polio when he was twenty, he became paralyzed from the neck down and had been living in the hospital for the last fifteen years in a huge machine that did his breathing for him. She tried to carry on a conversation with Bill. He could see her through a mirror that attached to a bracket on the front of the iron lung. It seemed Bill had a wall built around him from his years of disappointment in life. Bill only answered each question with a single syllable answer, and she found herself doing all the talking. The visit was difficult. She decided to try again the next week. This time he opened up a little more. She found out more about him. Bill was an avid reader and he had dreams to write a book, but he told her he had no knowledge of the mechanics of writing.

"You could take a correspondence course," Ann told him. "You can dictate to me and I'll type up the lessons and mail them." Once the course began Ann started visiting Bill every day. As they worked Ann saw Bill's confidence grow in his writing.

One day as Ann was visiting Bill another volunteer invited them both to a party. To Ann's surprise Bill accepted the invitation. Bill had to be strapped to a portable breathing device and taken on a stretcher. The whole thing terrified Ann, she was worried the whole time something would go wrong with the equipment. I want you to read the rest of this beautiful story in Ann's own words.

"Ann, will you marry me?"

My hands froze. So that was it! He had made this trip to show me he could safely leave the hospital.

In a daze I completed his belt adjustment and forced myself to speak. "I...uh...I really don't know how to answer, Bill." I stammered. "Give me a little time to think."

I could see the disappointment in his eyes. But then he bravely covered it up. "Don't take it to seriously, Ann...guess I had to much grape soda at the party."

In my apartment that night I could only think about Bill's proposal. One thing I knew: I loved him. Deeply, surely. For months now I had known it. And his proposal wasn't that much of a surprise.

In our visits I could feel Bill's fondness for me growing. I could see him reaching out for life and love after all his bitter years behind the walls of the hospital. He needed me and I loved him.

But could we manage? Did I have the courage to try?

Bill had many physical ailments, any one of which could lead to an emergency situation. From years in an iron lung, his joints had stiffened. His muscles sprained easily, and his bones were frail and brittle so that even giving him a bath took hours of gentle, slow handling.

A simple cold could develop into pneumonia. His breathing equipment broke down periodically and required immediate attention by a mechanic. Power failures were frequent in the area, we would have to live as close to the hospital as possible.

I would have to quit work and we would live on his Social Security disability checks and supplementary welfare. We would move into public housing.

I rose and walked to the window, looking into the rainy night. No, I couldn't do it. It was more than human strength could bear. The life God had asked Bill to accept for 15 years was too hard.

And then I looked back on my last 15 years; carefree, pointless, empty. And suddenly I knew I faced a decision. Life or death.

Marrying Bill would be accepting the cross, that is at the heart of all vital living. To be alive is to suffer sometimes. Suffering isn't all there is to life, but unless we accept misery as an integral part of it, all the other experiences are diminished. And suffering is unbearable

only when we feel alone in it.

So, I chose life, I chose Bill.

Ann chose the narrow path that led to life. She chose the path of suffering, but she chose the path to joy. She wrote this story nine years after she and Bill married, nine happy years. She had two roads in front of her to choose from and she chose the narrow one. She chose a life of hardship, but it led her to the highest mountain, to the greatest rewards. She also writes that Bill, her husband, published a book about his years in the hospital.

What Road Will You Choose?

Jesus chose a path of suffering in His life. Suffering can lead to a joy we never could have known any other way, an eternal joy. Jesus came to earth and chose a narrow path so we can have life and that was His joy to do. If we follow His example, we also will choose our paths wisely and bring life to ourselves and others. The first fork in the road is our salvation, it starts at the cross. As we continue down the narrow path, we face more choices in paths, remember Jesus chose the most difficult path, a death on a cross. He paved the way for us.

Remember also the narrow path leads to higher callings and a closer walk with the Lord. The narrowest path is the one Jesus walked. As you travel it, He will go with you.

Chapter Seven

Jesus Set His Face Like a Flint

"For the Lord God will help Me; Therefore, I will not be disgraced; Therefore, I have set My face like a flint, And I know that I will not be ashamed. Isaiah 50:7

Jesus was determined to go to the cross. He was determined to fulfill His destiny which was to become the sacrifice and atonement for our sins. This was a heavy load on Him. He once confided to His disciples. *"I came to send fire on the earth and how I wish it were already kindled! But I have a baptism to be baptized with, and how distressed I am until it is accomplished!" Luke 12:49-50* Jesus literally had the weight of the world on His shoulders.

Jesus' Life is about Purpose

Jesus had to stay focused on what his purpose was. He could not allow Himself to become sidetracked. He set his face like a flint, and He stayed on course. He purposed and determined to do what He came for.

Jesus knew His destiny was hard. He knew He had great suffering ahead, but He was focused and determined, and He did not waiver. Jesus' life was not about comfort or pleasure or seeking happiness. It was not about pleasing people who had other plans for Him, that were contrary to God's will.

He was disciplined; He went without sleep and would pray all night. He at one point fasted for forty days and nights while He stayed out in the desert and was tempted by Satan!! This does not sound like fun. Jesus' life was not about fun. There is something better than happiness and fun and that is fulfilling your purpose. Jesus fulfilled His purpose. It took great determination.

Staying Focused, The ABC's

You have a purpose, and it will take staying focused to fulfill that purpose. You may say, "I don't have a purpose," or "I don't know what my purpose is." You do have a purpose. God has made you for a distinct purpose that only you can fill, and maybe many purposes. There are people on this earth that you are meant to help.

If you have a spouse, a family or if you are a parent you have a huge God given purpose. I call it the A B C's, the basics. Your focus needs to be on your #1 priority, that is your walk with the Lord, your #2 priority if your married, is your spouse, {if you are not married your #2 priority IS NOT DATING} # 3 priority is your children, a huge priority, and #4 your home and or your job and your ministry. For some, the home is the job and some juggle both. Until you get these basic priorities down get everything else out of your life. Get focused. Get rid of distractions. Get your priorities straight.

For many years what serving the Lord meant to me was being a wife and mother, and it took all my effort. I had no time for anything else, and I mean no time. That was okay because I needed to focus on the ABC's. My attention was focused on those four priorities, and I juggled homemaking and a job.

I want to delve deeper into this subject because I see in our society right now, Christians included, that we have lost our purpose. Families have lost their purpose, serving the Lord and strengthening each other.

There are too many distractions; they have forgotten what is important. Husbands and wives seek things to bring themselves pleasure. Husbands spend their money on themselves instead of meeting the needs of their families. Mothers too, have become distracted, they have a baby and continue on with their busy lives just as before, leaving a hired person to do their job for their biggest job for them. Or whole families focus on entertainments rather than the purpose God had for them. We have too many distractions. We need to get back to the ABC's. We have to get rid of the junk in our lives, so we can achieve our purpose.

My purpose as a young wife and mother was to come through for and to be faithful to the people in my life, my husband and children.

This took all of me. This took focus. I remember years on end when my day started at one thirty a.m. That is what time I got up and went to work on my job, a paper route. I would get home between five thirty to seven thirty depending on the day. I went seven days a week, three hundred and sixty-five days a year. I worked this job so I could be home with my children when they needed me.

I would get my daughters off to school, drive my husband to work and then home school my son, because he had learning disabilities. Along with that I had the responsibility of the shopping, cooking and cleaning, going to the laundry mat and also the bill paying. Then picking up my husband from work and spending quality time teaching my kids about the Lord. I was busy all the time!!! It took focus, focusing on my priorities.

I remember I wanted to watch Perry Mason, it was an old show that came on in the afternoons, a mystery solver, show, I like those. I would start to watch it, but it would never fail, I would be needed. I longed to sit and watch it.

Sometimes purpose can seem mundane or hard or endless. It is not glamorous. Look at athletes who dream of the Olympics. They begin as children and train continually. They give up pleasures and free time because they are focused on a goal. They train for hours a day. That is what it takes. They have to get the junk out of their lives. They can't eat any old thing; they can't lay around.

They are focused on a goal, they have purpose. The pay-off comes for those who have purpose. An Olympic gold medal or a life faithfully lived that is pleasing to the Lord. These are pay offs.

Years after my children were raised, I was shopping at Wal-Mart, someone had given me some money and told me to get something for myself, I saw some Perry Mason DVD's and the Lord told me to buy them. I have never been one to watch much TV, and I wondered about watching all those DVD's.

The Lord let me know this was my time to watch Perry Mason. He let me sit around and watch them. He remembered me, He remembered something I gave up for the purpose He gave me, and He filled that small desire of my heart.

Each of us has responsibilities and purposes given to us by God for which we will have to give an account. We all have people we are responsible for or to. We all also have something to contribute to the body of Christ.

Avoid Emotional Pitfalls

I am concerned about families. I am concerned about children. I am concerned about the lack of focus people have toward God and their families. We need to set our face like a flint, like Jesus did. One huge trap I see to our focus, is emotional pitfalls. Our emotions cannot rule us. This is a trap of the devil, and it keeps us from our purpose.

There are times in our lives when we are especially susceptible to this. Some of those could be after a divorce, in a mid-life crisis situation or simply those who have never had their emotional needs met as a child.

We all have emotions, but we cannot let them rule us and we cannot let them steer us off our course with the Lord and with our God given responsibilities.

I have seen this recently in a friend who went through a divorce. It left her emotionally wounded and got her off course with her purpose.

I'll call her Sally. Sally suddenly had this huge emotional need after her divorce from an unfaithful husband. Now she had the burden of supporting her children and her children needed her attention more than ever. Sally had huge emotional needs, she felt empty. She immediately got on a dating website. This set her off on an emotional high as she began getting texts from interested suitors.

The problem was she forgot her ABC's. I noticed her children couldn't get her attention. She had her little smart phone going and her fingers whizzing away on the texting. She had a happy little grin as she would text this new suitor. Her children would be saying, "Mom, mom, mom MOM, MOM!!!" No answer. She was in another world. She went through several boyfriends and several emotional highs and lows, a lot of lows.

The problem was her house was a mess, her kids had no clean clothes to wear, her fridge was empty and she didn't get to the grocery store. Every day was a disaster. Not that Sally had it easy, but her focus was not on the ABC's, she was distracted. In between boyfriends she'd get a cat or a dog that she didn't have time to take care of to add to the confusion. Then a new love would bring a new emotional high, more distraction. She told me during a romance, "My life is just wonderful, everything is going wonderful."

I didn't see it that way at all. I saw her focused on the boyfriend, always on the texts, or the computer. She'd forget when to go to work, the house was a mess, and she had no patience with her kids.

Sally is not the only one with this problem. It sounds like Sally is a bad mother. She is not but she is distracted. She is on an emotional roller coaster, set off by her divorce, an emotional pitfall. I see many on this same track. Do I think that Sally should stay alone? Am I being too hard on her and others in her position?

I believe the answer is focus. Only God can meet our emotional needs, a million romantic relationships won't help. People caught on an emotional roller coaster for whatever reason need to set their course and focus and not follow their emotions.

This is hard but it can be done. Taking care of the kids, the house, the meals and the job is not as exciting as dating websites, but for single parents this is the course. Focus on the needs of each day. Look straight ahead. A new relationship that may present itself should be only in the peripheral part of your focus and only after the ABC's are established. The focus stays on God and children, if the new relationship does not hinder your focus but enhances it then it is okay but otherwise cut it off.

I have seen some who never get back on track and stay off emotionally, permanently. Their parents end up raising their children as they chase relationship after relationship. It is an emotional pitfall and a life poorly lived.

This is also true for those going through an emotional marriage crisis. An empty nest can cause an emotional pitfall. Then one of the spouses could be left void and be left susceptible to an emotional fling, I mean adultery. Set your course and don't follow your emotions. Don't go anywhere you shouldn't. Press into the Lord stay away from temptation and the way will clear again and you will fulfill your purpose. Following God means being faithful to your spouse. Set your face like a flint.

Even grief can be an emotional pit fall! We can't make grief a lifetime event. We have to get back to purpose. We all have a purpose.

There are many life events that can cause grief. Grief is part of healing, but don't stay there forever. Jesus set His face like a flint to finish His course. He wasn't ruled by His emotions. He faced other obstacles too.

Jesus Was Misunderstood

Jesus followed His purpose, but it took being misunderstood by everyone. It took only obeying one voice, God's. Jesus had to stand alone. His purpose and destiny were so much greater than those around Him believed. They wanted a king on earth; they wanted Him to free them from the Romans. Jesus was building an eternal, spiritual kingdom, which will never ever end. He did it by going to the cross. No one else saw it. Even after Jesus had risen from the dead and was about to ascend into Heaven the last thing the disciples said to Him was, *"Lord will you at this time restore the kingdom to Israel?"* They didn't get it.

I never realized just how much Jesus was misunderstood until I read the book The Archko Volume it is a book of archeological writings of the Sanhedrin and Talmuds of the Jews. It is a fascinating book.

In one of the writings the well-known Pharisee named Gamaliel is sent by the Sanhedrin to interview Jesus parents. Gamaliel lived during Jesus' time and he is written about in the book of Acts, chapter five, a speech he gives to the Jewish counsel is recorded there.

Before Jesus public ministry had begun, the Sanhedrin had sent Gamaliel to look into the facts of Jesus birth at which time he interviews Jesus' parents. I want to quote parts of this interview for you so you can see also how misunderstood Jesus was, even by his family. We start midway in Gamaliel's interview with Joseph, Jesus' earthly father.

I told him we had heard he had a vision, and I was sent to ascertain the facts in the case. He said he did not call it a vision; he called it a dream. He said after he and Mary agreed to marry, it seemed that something told him that Mary was with child; That he didn't know whether he was asleep or awake, but it made such an impression on his mind that he concluded to have nothing more to do with her; and while he was working one day under a shed, all at once a man in snowy white stood by his side, and told him not to doubt the virtue of Mary, for she was holy before the Lord; that the child conceived in her was not by man, but by the Holy Ghost, and that the child

would be free from human passions. In order to do this, he must- that is his humanity must- be of the extract of almah {that is the Hebrew word for virgin}, that he might endure all things and not resist, and fill the demands of prophecy. He said the angel told him that this child should be great and should rule all the kingdoms of this world. He said that this child should set up a new kingdom, wherein should dwell righteousness and peace, and that the kingdoms of this world which should oppose him, God would utterly destroy. I asked him, how could a virgin conceive of herself without the germination of the male? He said: "this is the work of God. He has brought to life the womb of Elizabeth, so she had conceived and will bear a son in her old age who will go before and tell of the coming of this King." After telling me these things, he disappeared like the melting down of a light. I then went and told Mary what had occurred, and she told me that the same angel, or one like him, had appeared to her and told the same things. So, I married Mary, thinking that if what the angel said was true, it would be greatly to our advantage; but I am fearful we are mistaken. Jesus seems to take no interest in us, nor anything else much. I call him lazy and careless. I don't think he will ever amount to much; much less be a king. If he does, he must do a great deal better than he has been doing.

Jesus was misunderstood by Joseph his earthly father. Joseph in this interview wanted Jesus to fit into a mold that he had, one of an earthly king. He totally misunderstood Jesus' purpose. He even says that Jesus being a king would be to his advantage. Joseph is thinking of his own personal gain. Later in the interview Gamaliel talks to Mary Jesus' mother. This is also very interesting, and she also misunderstands Jesus. I will quote more.

I asked her {Mary] if he was healthy; to give me a description of his life. She said he was perfectly healthy; that she never heard him complain of any pain or dissatisfaction; his food always agreed with him; that he would eat anything set before him, and if anyone else complained he would often say he thought it good enough, much better than we deserved. She said that Joseph was a little hard to please, but this boy had had answered him so often, and his answers were so mild and yet so suitable, that he had almost broken him of finding fault. She said he settled all the disputes of the family; that no odds what was the subject or who it was , one word from him closed all mouths, and what gave him such power was his words were always unpretending and spoken as though they were not intended as a rebuke, but merely as a decision. I asked her if she had ever seen him angry or out of humor. She said she had seen him apparently vexed and grieved at the disputes and follies of others but had never seen him angry. I asked her if he had any worldly aspiration after money or wealth, or a great name, or did he delight in fine dress, like most of the youth. She said that was one thing that vexed her, he seemed to take no care of his person; he did not care whether he was dressed or not, or whether the family got along well or ill; it was all alike to him. She said she talked to him about it, and he would look at her a little grieved and say 'woman [for such he always called me] you do not know who I am.' Indeed she said he takes so little interest in things of the world and great questions of the day, they were beginning to despair of his ever amounting to much- much less be a king, as the angel said he would be; if so, he would have to act very differently from what he was acting at that time.

Later in Gamaliel's summary he says, **"Thus it seems that Joseph and Mary have both lost all confidence in his becoming anything. They seem to think that the Sanhedrin should do something for him to get him out and let him show himself to the people.**

Jesus' mother and father totally misunderstood Him. They wanted Him to promote Himself. They thought of Him as a failure because He was not following what THEY THOUGHT His life should become. They were disappointed in Him. Jesus followed God's will for His life, and He was misunderstood by all the people in His life. There are times in my life I have felt this way too. Many have been misunderstood that follow the voice of God, like Jesus sometimes we walk alone.

I am going to quote a passage from the book, *God Calling,* a timeless best seller of prophetic writings. In this passage we get a little more insight on Jesus being misunderstood. The speaker is Jesus.

While I was on the earth, to the great number of those whom I came in contact, Mine was a lost cause. Even my disciples only believed, half doubting, half wondering. When they all forsook me and fled it was not so much fear of my enemies as the certainty that My Mission, however beautiful they thought it, had failed.

In spite of all I had taught them, in spite of the intimate revelation of the Last Supper, they had secretly felt sure that when the final moment came, and the

hatred of the Pharisees was openly declared against Me I should sound some call to action, and that I should lead My followers, and found My earthly kingdom. Even the disciples who had eyes to see My Spiritual Kingdom had thought that material forces had proved too strong for Me.

And then in another passage he says:

My overcoming was never, you know, for Myself, but for you, for My children. Each temptation, each difficulty I overcame as it presented itself. The powers of evil were strained to their utmost to devise means to break Me. They failed, but how they failed was known only to Me and to My Father, who could read my undaunted spirit. The world, even My own followers, would see a lost cause. Reviled, spat upon, scourged, they would deem Me conquered. How could they know My spirit was free, unbroken, unharmed? And so, as I had come to show man God, I must show him God unconquered, unharmed, untouched by evil and its power. Man could not see My spirit untouched, risen above these earth furies and hates, into the Secret Place of the Father. But man could see My Risen Body, and learn by that, that even the last attempt by man had been powerless to touch Me. Take heart from that for you must share My tribulations. If evil is to leave you unchallenged, you must be evil. If evil challenges you, if trials press sore, it is because you are on My side, and, as My friends, exposed to the hate of evil. But be of good cheer. You walk with Me. I conquered evil at every point, though man could only see it proved, beyond all doubt, when I rose from the dead. And in My conquering, you

walk unharmed today.

Yes, Jesus, our example, was misunderstood by men but He set his face like a flint and fulfilled his purpose, and His purpose was for us. God's plans are eternal and following Him and His plans may not be understood until eternity. Sometimes, we walk as Jesus did, alone and misunderstood. We must set our course and stay focused. But Jesus went before us, and He goes with us and we go in Him. Even we as a Body of Christ are totally misunderstood by the world. We cannot follow the thinking that accepts sin and breaks God's laws. We cannot follow worldly thinking which says there are many ways to God. We are viewed as narrow minded and mocked.

We can follow our example Jesus; He set His face like a flint. Fulfilling our purpose will take determination like Jesus had. We cannot be ruled by our emotions, there are emotional pitfalls that come throughout life, and we must hold our course by not being ruled by our emotions but by God and His word. It will take being misunderstood by many. Jesus was misunderstood but He stayed on track. He set His face like a flint and so can we.

Chapter Eight
Jesus Stayed in Peace and was Content

"Come to Me, all you who labor and are heavy laden, and I will give you rest. Take My yoke upon you and learn from Me, for I am gentle and lowly in heart, and you will find rest for your souls." Matthew 11: 28 -29

Jesus walked in peace and was content. He calls Himself gentle and lowly in heart. Not only is Jesus our example of peace, He is the source of our peace. We see in many of Jesus' words and actions evidence of his inner peace. We also see contentment. We will discuss this after we discuss

His peace.

Jesus Sleeps in A Boat During A Storm

I want to quote you this passage because it is so amazing to me.

Now when He got into a boat His disciples followed Him. And suddenly a great tempest arose on the sea, so that the boat was covered with the waves. But He was asleep. Then His disciples came to Him and awoke Him saying, "Lord save us! We are perishing!" But He said to them, "Why are you fearful, O you of little faith?" Then He arose and rebuked the winds and the sea. And there was great calm. Matthew 8:23-26

There are two things about Jesus that amaze me in this scripture. Number one is, how could He sleep so soundly in a sinking boat in the middle of a terrible storm? Could you? Good sound sleep is a result of a peaceful heart. Jesus heart was so at rest He could sleep in such a storm in which the disciples yelled that they were dying!

I remember just before I was saved at the age of fourteen, I was extremely troubled, and it showed up in my sleep. I would wake up in the living room or the kitchen tripping over something. I would wander in my sleep and it would scare me. I had no peace at any time, not even in my sleep. I was afraid to go to sleep because I was worried, I was going to wake up outside in the road. It was during this time Jesus saved me and the sleep walking stopped. I have never had that trouble again.

The immediate thing I noticed in the first seconds after I called out to God and He saved me was that the constant turbulent feelings I had were gone and I felt this amazing thing called peace. My soul had been like the turbulent sea and as I encountered Jesus, I too had a great calm. Jesus is full of peace and an encounter with Him brings peace. Jesus has such a strong sense of peace He could sleep in a sinking ship! I find this amazing, and I want it too!

The second thing I find so interesting is that fact that Jesus acts like it is completely natural NOT to fear and to have peace and He asks, *"Why are you so fearful, O you of little faith?"* They were fearful because they were in a sinking ship in a great tempest, or an awful storm!!! They said they were dying! {or perishing} This was serious. Jesus has such faith in God His peace never waivers.

We see this attitude again in Jesus' sermon about worry. I will mention it rather than quote it in Matthew 6:25-34. Jesus keeps asking, "Why do you worry?" He says God feeds the birds and clothes the grass of the field, won't He take care of you? He also tells us not to worry about tomorrow.

I would like to live like that! I am not there yet. Not even close. I live in Northern Michigan and my job keeps me driving all day. I am a home health aide. I check the weather in the winter several times a day and when I see snow in the forecast coming up, I start to worry days in advance. I get myself in a tizzy! Is driving in a winter storm worse than being in a sinking boat on the Sea of Galilee during a tempest? No, I have a long way to go.

Psalms 46 tells us, *God is our refuge and strength, a*

very present help in trouble, Therefore we will not fear, though the earth be removed, and though the mountains be carried into the midst of the sea; though its waters roar and be troubled, though the mountains shake with its swelling.

Peace in Jesus

Peace in every situation is this really possible, to leave fear worry and stress or even terror behind? If you have peace, how can you keep it? The Bible tells us *Be anxious for nothing but in everything by prayer and supplication, with thanksgiving, let your requests be made known to God; and the peace of God which surpasses all understanding, will guard your hearts and minds through Christ Jesus. Philippians 4:6-7* If you are holding onto peace then you are holding onto victory. The peace of God guards your heart and your mind. Satan will not like it if you are in peace because he cannot get you. He will attack that peace. Don't let him.

One of my biggest obstacles to peace has been that I always have something to worry about.

I think like this, I have a new patient on Friday I feel kind of nervous about that as soon as Friday is over, I will have peace. Then next comes a snowstorm in the forecast on a day I have to drive a lot. I say to myself as soon as I get through this snowstorm, I will be okay, then something else comes up, maybe a meeting with my supervisor here comes the nerves again,

Peace is now. Jesus had peace in the midst of the storm, and He spoke peace to the storm. His victory was in the peace. We need to have peace in this moment. Jesus told us in *Matthew 6:34 "Therefore do not worry about tomorrow, for tomorrow will worry about its own things. Sufficient for the day is its own trouble."*

We can only handle one day at a time, and we need to handle it with prayer and stay in peace. When our peace leaves us, we need to stop, find when it left, pray, and pick it up again. If you have trouble then it's time to start practicing, reread Philippians 4;6-7 and start practicing peace.

Jesus Was Content

Paul said something powerful and I believe Jesus lived this way, Paul learned it from Him. It was about contentment which I believe goes hand in hand with peace.

I have learned whatever state I am in, to be content: I know how to be abased, and I know how to abound. Everywhere and in all things, I have learned to be full and to be hungry, both to abound and to suffer need. I can do all things through Christ who strengthens me. Philippians 4:11-13

This state of mind is new to me, to be content in every situation. This is mature Christianity, it is not shallow stuff. Contentment does not need to depend on your current situation, but your attitude toward your life and most of all toward God.

I want to requote a portion of the passage I quoted in the last chapter from *The Archko Volume.* This is in the passage in which Gamaliel is interviewing Mary, Jesus'

mother, about Jesus disposition. We can see in it, Jesus
has learned to be content.

**I asked her if he was healthy; to give a description
of his life. She said that he was perfectly healthy; that she
never heard him complain of any pain or dissatisfaction;
his food always agreed with him, and if anyone else
complained he would often say he thought it was good
enough, much better than we deserved.**

We get a little clue of His day-to-day life here. He is
thankful for what He has. He does not complain even if it is
not so good. Jesus is not chasing fleshly desires He is
content with what He has. How could Jesus do this? We
get a clue in John chapter four where Jesus is talking with
the woman at the well.

Jesus and the Woman at the Well

*So He came to a city of Samaria which is called
Sychar, near the plot of ground that Jacob gave to his son
Joseph. Now Jacob's well was there. Jesus, therefore, being
wearied from the journey, sat thus by the well. It was
about the sixth hour. A woman of Samaria came to draw
water. Jesus said to her, "Give Me a drink." For His
disciples had gone to the city to buy food. John 4:4-8*

We see here is Jesus and He is tired, hungry and
thirsty and the disciples are out getting the food. The next
part of this story Jesus ministers to this woman. She is a
lost sheep, a woman who'd had five husbands and the one
she was with wasn't even her husband. Jesus ministers to
her and she runs off to tell her whole town the Messiah

was here. Meanwhile the disciples return with the food.

> *In the meantime, His disciples urged Him saying, "Rabbi eat." But He said to them, "I have food to eat which you do not know." Therefore, the disciples said to one another, "Has anyone brought Him something to eat?" Jesus said, "My food is to do the will of Him who sent Me and to finish His work." John 4:31-34*

We are getting a little clue why Jesus is not fazed by things like hunger, thirst and being tired. Why He is content whether He has them or not. Jesus was hungry here, but something was so much more important to Him. It was doing God's will, doing spiritual things, unseen things. Jesus' contentment isn't in earthly things. Yes, He had to eat to live here, like we all do, but He is content with whatever is set before Him whether delicious or pretty bad. His delight is in doing God's will. It is food to Him.   His contentment isn't rooted in the things of this world. I want to quote to you another passage from a favorite book of mine that will show us another amazing example of how truly commendable this attitude is toward God.

A Homeless Man Becomes a Great King in Heaven

This passage is from the book *The Final Quest*. I talk about this story in just about every book I write, because it changed my life and my way of thinking. The book is a prophetic vision the author Rick Joyner had. In this portion of the book Rick is being shown those in the heavenly realm called the overcomers. They are those who lived their lives to the fullest for God on the earth and are very great in the kingdom of heaven. In this passage I will quote, Rick meets a homeless man who is one of the greatest in the kingdom of heaven, and he is a king.

This homeless man's name is Angelo, and he has had a very difficult life. He was born deaf, to abusive parents, who kept him locked in an attic with very little care. He was there until age eight when the authorities discovered him and put him in a mental institution. There the abuse continued. Then he was turned out on the streets and was homeless. Although this man had a miserable life, he overcame, by using all the love God had placed in him to overcome, and his life was VERY pleasing to God. In this passage Rick is having a conversation with Jesus about Angelo's life. Rick had seen this man in a vision years before, and he now is surprised to learn he was a real person. Jesus tells Rick that Angelo died a martyr, and this blows Rick's mind, why Angelo was considered a martyr and why Angelo was so pleasing to God. In Rick's mind it doesn't add up. I want to quote you this passage about Angelo, an abused homeless man. It is one of the most touching things I have ever read in my life. The Lord is explaining to Rick why Angelo is considered a martyr.

"Angelo was so faithful with the little that I had given to him, I gave him three more portions of my love. He used all of that to quit stealing. He almost starved, but he refused to take anything that was not his. He bought his food with what he could make collecting bottles, and occasionally finding someone who would let him do yard

work. He could not hear but he had learned to read, so I sent him a gospel tract. As he read it the Spirit opened his heart, and he gave his life to Me. I again doubled the portions of My love to him and he faithfully used all of them. He wanted to share Me with others, but he could not speak. Even though he lived in such poverty, he started spending over half of everything he made on gospel tracts to give out on street corners."

"How many did he lead to you?" I asked, thinking that it must have been multitudes for him to be sitting with the kings.

"One," the Lord answered. *"I let him lead a dying alcoholic to Me to encourage him. It encouraged him so much he would have stood on that corner for many more years just to bring another soul to repentance. But all of heaven was entreating Me to bring him here, and I, too, wanted him to receive his reward."*

"But what did he do to become a king?" I asked.

"He was faithful with all he was given; he overcame all until he became like Me, and he died a martyr."

"But what did he overcome, and how was he martyred?"

"He overcame the world with My love. Very few have overcome so much with so little. Many of My people dwell in homes that kings would have envied just a century ago because of their conveniences, but do not appreciate them, while Angelo would so appreciate a cardboard box on a cold night that he would turn it into a glorious temple of My presence. He began to love everyone and everything. He would rejoice more over an

apple than some do over a great feast. He was faithful with all that I gave him, even though it was not very much compared to what I gave others, including you.

A little later in the story the Lord tells Rick how Angelo died.

"He froze to death trying to keep an old wino alive who had passed out in the cold.

"Lord, I know that he is truly an overcomer," I remarked. "And it is so just for him to be here. But are those who die that way also considered martyrs?"

"Angelo was a martyr every day that he lived. He would only do enough for himself to stay alive, and he gladly sacrificed his life to save a needy friend. As Paul wrote to the Corinthians, even if you give your body to be burned, but do not have love, it counts as nothing. But when you give yourself with love it counts for much. Angelo died every day because he did not live for himself, but for others."

There is a lot of mind-blowing information in this passage, but I want you to see this, that Angelo, a homeless man, that slept in a cardboard box and barely had food, was filled with gratitude to God and he was content with what he had!

He was not only grateful and content with very little, but he also shared what he had. I want you to get a glimpse of how pleasing this attitude is to God. This homeless man has so pleased God he will be a great king for all eternity.

Angelo truly became Christ like, he truly followed Jesus' example. Did you notice the part of the passage that said Angelo spent half of his very meager income buying gospel tracts? Angelo like Jesus was motivated by the work of the kingdom.

So many of us totally miss the mark when it comes to truly following Jesus, I am including myself. We read the gospels but totally overlook the life that Jesus led, the words He spoke and His attitude. This homeless man, Angelo really got it. He used all the love God had put in his heart. He wasn't afraid to be cold or hungry; he was more concerned with pleasing God. He even gave up his life trying to keep an old wino alive that was passed out and freezing to death. Somehow hunger and cold were not as important to Angelo as helping others. He had the same motivation that Jesus had when He was at the well in our Bible story.

I believe a huge secret to peace and contentment is to truly put doing God's will first, like Jesus did, like Angelo did. The motivation for this is love, love for God and love for others. This attitude allowed Angelo to live in such a way that the Lord referred to him as a martyr every day that he lived! It was Jesus' attitude the same attitude that kept Him on a Cross, to pay for our sins.

The Children of Israel are Discontent

Let's flip this thing and look at it from the opposite standpoint. How does God view those who are discontent? We find a perfect example of this in the book of Numbers in chapter eleven. The children of Israel are discontent.

Most people know the story of Moses and the children of Israel. The children of Israel were slaves in Egypt and living in terrible conditions. They cried out to

God for deliverance. God spoke to Moses in the burning bush and told him to go tell the Pharaoh to let the people go. Never had a group of people in any time see such miracles! God delivered the people of Israel in such a mighty way. They saw plagues that came on the Egyptians but not on themselves, plagues of frogs and darkness and boils and the water turning to blood and many more all at the command of Moses. Finally, the last plague all the first born in Egypt died. At last, they were let go. Then came the big miracles, when the Egyptians chased them, and the Red Sea parted, and they walked through the middle of the sea on dry ground!

I would love to have seen that! That was only the beginning, they had water come from rocks, their shoes and clothes never wore out, they were led by God Himself in a pillar of cloud by day and fire by night. The miracles just kept on coming! God even fed them in the desert; He sent them manna to gather. It was some sort of stuff that sounded good tasting to me.

Wouldn't you think these people who were so miraculously saved from their oppressors and saw more miracles than any other generation would be grateful and content? No, they whined and complained to God because they wanted meat to eat. They wished they were back in Egypt for the food! So, the Lord sent them quail to eat, but the Bible tells us, *But while the meat was still between their teeth, before it was chewed, the wrath of the Lord was aroused against the people, and the Lord struck the people with a very great plague. Numbers 11:33*

Their attitude definitely was displeasing to the Lord. We see how important an attitude of contentment is. After all God had done for the children of Israel they wanted to go back for some meat! The wrath of the Lord was aroused.

Can we learn to be content as Paul said, no matter what our situation is? Can we make the things that are important to God our priority and be thankful for the provisions He gives us?

How about peace, can we be at peace today and leave tomorrow in God's hands? Peace is so valuable, it protects us from the devil, and peace guards our hearts and minds. What people wouldn't give for peace? Jesus is our source of peace. We see He had peace by trusting God and walking in contentment because He was focused on eternal things. Angelo followed Jesus in this way. A man who had nothing learned peace and contentment with the very little he had. Angelo was an overcomer; he followed his great example, Jesus.

Chapter Nine
Servants Be Submissive

Servants be submissive to your masters with all fear, not only to good and gentle, but also to the harsh. 1 Peter 2:18

Oh, did I hate that verse. That is so contrary to my way of thinking. Not just mine. Every movie we see, in our world, every plot and story are giving us a message, and this is not the message.

My husband has watched his action movies for years. I would see them playing in our living room, even though I never really sat down and watched them with him. I have seen enough of enough of them to get the plot and the plot was always the same.

It always started with our all-around good guy not looking for any trouble and then some evil villain kills his wife or girlfriend, and sometimes even a child. {These movie writers really know how to mess with a man's emotions.} That would only be the beginning of this poor guys troubles, but from that point on my husband's, {and every other man watching the movie} need for revenge is being fed and then it grows from there to a climax, until our poor action hero being pushed to such a point he becomes enraged with righteous vindication and fights or shoots until he completely destroys this hideous villain who unleashed such an attack. And every man watching is cheering on the violence because his manly emotions have been stretched to the limit to protect his loved ones. And somewhere in the movie our hero has picked up a new babe to protect, usually a beautiful blonde.

Same plot, sometimes even the same actor, over and over, my husband eats that stuff up. It is the revenge scenario. It plays on a man's inner drive to protect his family and feeds him with a desire to beat to a pulp anyone who messes with him.

We see the same messages in women's and children's movies but in a modified way for our tastes, but it is still revenge and not humility, the idea of submission is still foreign to us.

How about the master part of that verse? Be submissive to your master. Thankfully our society no longer allows slavery; it has become repulsive to us. I can hardly stand to watch any movie about slavery, but I have seen a few, and I have read some books, true stories about slavery and cried my way through them. The evil done to people through slavery is beyond comprehension and I have the same desire for revenge reading them as my husband in his action movies.

Again, thankfully we have abolished slavery, but we

all have been in positions where someone in authority over us has abused us, mistreated us, or taken advantage of us. A supervisor at work, a teacher, or for a child a babysitter, the police, the government, the list goes on. This verse is still relevant for us today, very relevant. And it is still the opposite of our human nature. We want revenge.

Let's read further in our passage of scripture. *For this is commendable, if because of conscience toward God one endures grief, suffering wrongfully. For what credit is it if, when you are beaten for your faults, you take it patiently? But when you do good and you suffer for it, if you take it patiently, this is commendable before God.*

I want to step in here and say how wrong this verse still rubbed me because I don't even like the idea of being beaten for my faults let alone doing good and suffering. I have always been one to deceive myself into the fact I wasn't wrong, about anything, and I never want to suffer for any reason right or wrong. {Are you getting some idea about what an emotional mess I am.}

But I have to tell you I really HATED this scripture. Let's read on. *For to this you were called, because Christ also suffered for us, leaving us an example you should follow His steps. "Who committed no sin, Nor was any guile found in His mouth", who when He was reviled did not revile in return; when he suffered He did not threaten, but committed Himself to Him who judges righteously; who Himself bore ur sins in His own body on a tree, that we having died to sins, might live for righteousness—by whose stripes you were healed. 1Peter 2:19-24.*

I don't believe in slavery but yet here in scripture it

126

is telling slaves to be obedient to their masters, even those that mistreat them. Being submissive and respecting authority is huge, in scripture. The key here is not to do nothing. The key is to do the right thing and that is to be submissive and to commit your soul unto God. This is an act of faith.

We need to see in every situation of abuse and mistreatment, the real force behind it is Satan. It is the devil persecuting you and he is using the person that is abusing their authority. Jesus was falsely accused, by the Jewish authorities. Jesus was brought before the human court and mistreated. Jesus had the ability to stop His abusers, but He submitted to human authority. We are told in this verse He did not revile in return.

This would have multiplied the evil. Anytime we react to evil with revenge or anger we multiply its power. Jesus defeated Satan. He defeated Satan for us and He left us an example for us to defeat Satan as He did. He submitted to the ungodly authority but committed Himself to God's hands. Instead of evil being multiplied it was totally defeated.

David and Saul

King David also was a perfect example of submission to an evil authority, King Saul. David, a young shepherd boy was a faithful subject of King Saul. After David killed the giant, Goliath, Saul became jealous of David's popularity with the people and tried to kill David.

For years Saul relentlessly chased David down to kill him, but David would not fight back or lay a hand on him. He had to keep fleeing but he chose not to lay a hand on Saul, he left him to God.

One time as Saul was pursuing David; he came after David with three thousand men. David and his men were hiding in a cave. Saul came into the cave alone to go to the bathroom. David's men urged David to kill Saul, but David refused to. While Saul was in there David sneaked up behind him and cut off part of his garment.

When Saul returned to his men David came out of the cave and called to Saul, *"My lord the king!" And when Saul looked behind him, David stooped with his face to the earth and bowed down. And David said to Saul: "Why do you listen to the words of men, who say, 'Indeed David seeks to do you harm'? Look this day your eyes have seen that the Lord delivered you into my hand in the cave, and someone urged me to kill you. But my eye spared you, and I said, "I will not stretch out my hand against the Lord's anointed.' "Moreover, my father see! Yes, see the corner of your robe in my hand! For in that I cut off the corner of your robe and did not kill you. Yet you hunt my life to take it. Let the Lord judge between you and me, and let the Lord avenge me on you. But my hand shall not be against you. As the proverb of the ancients says, 'Wickedness proceeds from the wicked.' But my hand shall not be against you." 1 Samuel 24:8-13*

King David practiced this same principle of submission. He did not return evil for evil, but he committed himself to the Righteous Judge, God. In time Saul was killed in a battle and David became king. {David actually mourned Saul's death; he loved his enemy.} David did not promote himself, God promoted him.

God does not want us to fall into Satan's hands. He does not want the things Satan does to us, through others, to enslave us to bitterness, hatred and unforgiveness, which will cause us to perpetuate evil and to be defeated by Satan. If we behave like Jesus and David, the problem becomes God's and He will handle the situation.

Handling the Situation Correctly

This reminds me of a story I read in a little book I read one time called, *One Man's Faith and Miracles,* by Alvin "Mike" Martin. It is a book about a man who stepped out in faith and began a wonderful ministry for young people. He lived and operated his own finances and the ministry he had by faith. His ministry needed printing equipment and the Lord spoke to Mike and told He would provide printing equipment for the ministry.
Mike went to see some printing equipment in a printing shop that was for sale. A man there showed Mike the complete printing equipment and quoted Mike a price. Mike felt the Holy Spirit witness that this was the equipment He wanted them to have. Mike tried to raise the money and couldn't and the Lord told Him to trust Him. I want to quote the rest of the story for you.

About one week later I went downtown and stopped in a small printing shop which belonged to a Mrs. Marie Spidell, in Seattle, to have some printing done. I had never been in her place before. As I came in the door she said, "The Lord told me I am to give you my printing equipment."

Surprise followed by great joy came to my heart. I

thought, of course, that it was in the shop I was in, but handing me a piece of paper, she said, "I have another printing shop at this address, and the equipment that the Lord told me to give you for your work is located there." I looked at the address with amazement, for it was the same address where we had looked at the presses on that afternoon when the Holy Spirit had witnessed to us that this was the equipment, He was giving us.

I went from there to the other shop and again talked with the man who wanted to sell us Mrs. Spidell's presses. I asked him who owned the presses and he told me Mrs. Spidell did. I had assumed the presses belonged to him. I then told him I had just seen Mrs. Spidell and she had given us this complete printing shop for King's Teens. Instead of rejoicing with me the man became angry about it. Perplexed I left him.

Shortly thereafter a friend of mine told me that he had seen this man and he had accused us of stealing these presses from him. I was shocked to hear this. I went up to see the man alone and pointing to the presses still in his shop, I asked "Did you tell people I had stolen these presses from you?" He hedged a bit, but he did not say "Yes" or "no". I then told him I would go to Mrs. Spidell and get everything straightened up. He then said, "No, it's O.K. I am sorry."

I then thought everything was straightened out, but later I heard from other people who had just talked with this printer, and they told me that he had accusingly said I had stolen the presses he was using in his shop.

The word of God says, in Matthew 18:15-17, "Moreover if thy brother shall trespass against thee, go and tell him his fault between thee and him alone: if he shall hear thee, thou hast gained thy brother. But, if he will not hear thee, then take with thee one or two more, that in the mouth of two or three witnesses every word may be established. And if he shall neglect to hear them, tell it unto the church."

Mike goes on to tell us in the story how he did what scripture said he went back twice to the man once with two witnesses, one being Mrs. Spidell and next with men from the church. Mike chose to submit to God's word in this situation and to humble himself before this man. In this way, Mike followed Christ's example and continued to reach out in love to this man who still continued to tell people he had stolen the presses. The story ends this way.

Sometime later, after we had taken the presses to our own shop, I went down to see Mrs. Spidell again, and as I came into her shop, this same printer was visiting with her. I immediately put out my hand and said, "Brother I want everything to be completely straight between us so that you will love me in the Lord. I have nothing in my heart against you."

He would not return my love or make friends with me. I could do nothing else except leave with my heart heavy. When the man left Mrs. Spidell's printing shop just a few minutes later, he fell over dead in the street.

The man fell over dead! Mike did everything he could to win this man. Mike had submitted to authority [scripture] which put the situation totally in God's hands. This man continued to lie about the presses, saying that Mike had stolen them. Mike handled the situation correctly, he became submissive and did not seek revenge, the authority Mike was submissive to was God, through His word, which seeks reconciliation, but this printer hardened his heart and refused to stop lying about him or become friends. Because of this, this man, the printer, was not coming against Mike but against God. Although this man received several chances his heart was hardened, and he came to a dramatic end.

My point here is committing something to God is not doing nothing; it is leaving the matter to God as the scripture said but *committed Himself to Him who judges righteously.* We don't engage ourselves in the human conflict that Satan throws at us, which would cause Satan to win, but we follow the example of Jesus, and we leave the judgment to God. This is the correct way to handle the situation.

Following Jesus example when we are punished for doing the right thing is the way to ultimately defeat the devil in the situation. We are to be submissive to those who mistreat us and follow scripture.

King David was also a perfect example of this. It put him in a terrible position because Saul tried to kill him over and over. But David handled the situation correctly and came out victorious.

This goes against everything we learn in the world about getting revenge, but revenge only multiplies evil, submission to God defeats the devil and wins us the victory.

Chapter Ten
Faith Pleases Jesus

But the just shall live by faith Habakkuk 2:4

One of my all-time favorite Bible teachers, writer and speaker, Kenneth Hagin wrote that faith is the most important subject in the Bible. I will quote his book,

Why Is Faith So Important

Faith is the most important subject in the whole Bible. A preacher asked me one time, "Brother Hagin, you know I have been preaching for years, and I never preached on the subject of faith yet. Why do you preach on it so much?"

I said, "Because a man who had never preached on faith has never preached the Bible. There's not anything in the Bible as important as this subject. You cannot even be saved without faith, because...'*by grace you are saved through FAITH; and that not of yourselves it is the gift of God' Ephesians 2:8*

I continued; You can't live for God without faith. You can't please God without faith, because the Bible says....'*without faith it is impossible to please Him...Hebrews 11:6.* The Bible also says '....*we walk by faith not by sight' 2 Corinthians 5:7.*

"The Christian walk is a faith walk," I told him. "You can't fight spiritual battles without faith because the Bible says the only fight, we are supposed to fight is the fight of faith. It says,' *Fight the good fight of faith'"* 1 Timothy6:12

When I gave that fellow all those scriptures, he just stood there and sort of blinked his eyes.

"Man!" he said, "I'd better get to preaching faith, hadn't I?"

I said, "Yeah you sure had."

The late Kenneth Hagin is one of the most respected and notable teachers on faith. I have devoured all his books on faith and read them over and over. If faith is so important, we need to find out more about it, and use it.

Jesus Is Impressed by Faith

I have noticed in the in the gospels that the way to impress Jesus was through faith. He loved it when someone had faith, it delighted Him. He always commended those with great faith, and they always got what they wanted from Him. Let us look at a few people who came to Jesus in faith.

Now when Jesus had entered Capernaum a centurion came to Him, pleading with Him, saying, "Lord my servant is lying at home paralyzed, dreadfully tormented." And Jesus said, "I will come and heal him."

The centurion answered and said, "Lord I am not worthy that You should come under my roof. But only speak a word and my servant will be healed. For I also am a man under authority, having soldiers under me. And I say to this one 'Go' and he goes; and to another 'Come' and he comes; and to my servant "Do this' and he does it.

When Jesus heard it he marveled, and said to those that followed, "Assuredly I say to you, I have not found such great faith, not even in Israel!" Matthew 8: 5-13

Did you noticed it said Jesus marveled at the centurion's faith? Then He turned and addressed the crowd, telling them that this was the greatest faith He had seen, even in Israel. Remember Jesus has been around forever, and this was the greatest faith he had seen. If they gave out Emmy awards for the most faith ever, the centurion, a despised Roman soldier gets the prize! This man really impressed Jesus and that is how you impress Jesus, with faith.

We receive from God, by faith, and only by faith. I have learned that whining and complaining doesn't work. Faith works. Let's look at another example of great faith.

And behold, a woman of Canaan came out from that region and cried out to Him, saying, "Have mercy on me, O Lord Son of David! My daughter is severely demon possessed."

But He answered her not a word. And His disciples came and urged Him, saying "Send her away, for she cries out after us."

But He answered and said, "I was not sent except to the lost sheep of the house of Israel."

Then she came and worshipped Him, saying, "Lord, help me!"

But He answered and said, "It is not good to take the children's bread and throw it to the little dogs."

And she said, "True Lord, yet even the little dogs eat the crumbs which fall from their master's table."

Then Jesus answered and said to her' "O woman, great is your faith! Let it be to you as you desire." And her daughter was healed from that very hour. Matthew 15:22-28

I used to think Jesus was being mean to her and I couldn't understand it, then I changed my mind, I have decided Jesus was seeing how determined she was, how tenacious her faith was. She definitely passed the test; she was not going to take "No" for an answer. Then Jesus gave her a huge compliment. {Remember its faith that He likes} He says, "Woman great is your faith!"

This woman, another foreigner, thrilled Jesus. He loves faith. She was persistent and faith is persistent.

Is this okay? Is it okay to grab onto God and not let go until you get what you came for? Yes, she got what she wanted; her child was set free. Yes, it is okay to be determined, to use your faith and not let go. Faith does not take no for answer, faith hangs on. God loves faith! This woman didn't just have faith, she had great faith. She was commended by Jesus. We need what she's got!

On the other hand, we see Jesus get absolutely disgusted and almost angry at those who displayed a lack of faith. You will notice the adjectives Jesus uses with the lack of faith, perverse and adulterous. How can you get any worse than that?

And when they had come to the multitude a man came to Him, kneeling down to Him saying, "Lord have mercy on my son, for he is an epileptic and suffers severely; for he often falls into the fire and often into the water. So, I brought him to Your disciples, but they could not cure him."

Then Jesus answered and said, "O Faithless and perverse generation, how long shall I be with you? How long shall I bear with you? Bring him here to Me." Matthew 17:14-17

Jesus gets upset with unbelief. You get nowhere with Him with unbelief. You will get Him mad. Then there were those who took unbelief a step further. After all the miracles Jesus performed, they had the nerve to come and ask Jesus for a sign. This did not go over well with Him.

Then the Pharisees and Sadducees came and testing Him asked that He show them a sign from heaven. He answered and said to them, "When it is evening you say, 'It will be fair weather, for the sky is red"; and in the morning, "it will be foul weather today for the sky is red and threatening.' Hypocrites! You know how to discern the face of the sky, but you cannot discern the signs of the times. A wicked and adulterous generation seeks after a sign, and no sign shall be given to it except the sign of the prophet Jonah." And He left them and departed. Matthew 16:1-4

Jesus called them wicked and adulterous and walked away. We don't impress Jesus with unbelief! Faith is very important, and we need to live by it, we need to find out more about it and use it. This next verse gives us more insight into faith.

But without faith it is impossible to please Him, for he who comes to God must believe that He is, and that He is a rewarder of those who diligently seek Him. Hebrews 11:6

I believe that the basis for all faith is simply to believe that God is good! That God loves you, and you can trust Him! There is also another clue in this verse in Hebrews 6:11 If your faith is not working ask yourself, "Am I diligently seeking Him?" The verse says He rewards those who diligently seek Him.

Summer uses Diligence

I have had times when I have decided to pray until I get an answer and I refuse to give up. One time I did this although it seems silly now; but I was really upset at the time. It was about a Christmas present. This was back when we were really poor. We didn't have much. Our family had gotten together and got me and Jim a gas grill. It was all we got that year, of course, because it was an expensive item.

I went through a lot of emotions over that gas grill. I couldn't figure out why they got it for us. I had so many things I needed and wanted, and I got something I didn't want that was expensive. Maybe you have to have been really poor to realize the pity party I was going through.

Well, I decided I better try to like it and I did. Hot dogs tasted pretty good grilled on that thing.

About a month after Christmas, I went out with a pack of hotdogs to cook on this new grill.

It wouldn't work.

Oh, did that upset me! This was all I got for Christmas and now the thing would not work!

I wasn't taking this. I sat down on the front stoop next to that grill and started praying. I was not going to stop praying until God fixed my grill!

About a half hour later I was still praying. I meant it; I told God I was not moving until He did something. I kept trying the grill and it still didn't work. I kept it up.

As I was sitting there praying, I noticed a big Mexican man across that lived across the street and down. I didn't know him, but I had seen him before. He came out and started working in his yard.

The Lord spoke, "Go ask him to look at your grill."

I did not want to; I was a little scared of him. But I had been praying a long time and I was determined, so I nervously went over and asked the man if he could look at my grill. He did and he fixed it. I never would have figured it out on my own.

I know I was being a little over emotional about that grill because it was all I had gotten, and I wanted other things, but God understands that. He honored my diligence, and He helped me again. Faith is diligent. I sat there praying for quite a while, determined.

Our foreign woman, in Matthew 15, was diligently seeking Him, the disciples thought she was irritating; she was calling out to Him. They wanted Jesus to get rid of her.

I would call that diligence. Then, she worshipped Him, and she refused to be turned away. She knew who Jesus was, so did the centurion. They both knew Jesus had the power and authority to help them, they knew He was the Messiah. She knew Jesus was her only hope for her daughter to be healed. Who is our only hope? If all our hope is in Jesus, we like the woman, and the centurion are on the right track. We can be like them, we can be diligent, we can know who He is, we can come to Him with our faith, and we can refuse to give up. That is faith.

Chapter Eleven
Holiness

Therefore gird up the loins of you mind, be sober and rest your hope fully upon the grace that is to be brought to you at the revelation of Jesus Christ; as obedient children, not conforming yourselves to the former lusts, as in your ignorance; but as He who has called you is holy, you also be holy in all your conduct, because it is written, "Be holy, for I am holy." 1Peter 1:13-15

I don't know what kind of picture the word holiness conjures up in your mind but for a lot of us it's grim. It is a list of dos and don'ts. It is no make-up, long dresses and straight hair. It seems blah. Let's get that out of our minds.

We all have a sin problem. We were born with a sin problem. We come from a fallen race of people who are spiritually dead, and we need redemption. Jesus met our need on the cross. We are saved through faith in Him. We become righteous through faith in Him. Our spirit is reborn; we become one with Him in our spirit. His righteousness is our righteousness. But just like any birth this is just the beginning. What happens next? Are we supposed to never sin again? What if we do, will God now reject us? How good do I have to be? Can I really be holy?

What Is Holiness?

Before Jesus came to earth, God through Moses gave us His laws, the Ten Commandments. There were more than the Ten Commandments, there were lots of instructions about sacrifices and such and there were listed things called abominations which were not to be tolerated at all. These were things like idolatry, witchcraft, gross sex sins, and child sacrifice.

When Jesus came to earth, He raised the bar. He did this in the Sermon on the Mount, we can read it in Matthew chapters 5, 6 and 7. Now, He tells us not only can we not commit murder but if we are angry with our brother and call him a fool, we are in danger of hell fire.

He told us not only can we not commit adultery, that if we look at some lustfully, we have already committed adultery in our hearts. He tells us our charitable deeds must be done in secret or we have already received our rewards.

Holiness is now not only a matter of our deeds but

a matter of our hearts! Not only are our deeds to be holy but our thoughts and our words as well. Is this kind of holiness even possible? Should we just give up now because we know we can never attain this, is He just asking too much?

God Will Meet You Where You Are

I have some good news for you. Jesus did it for us on the cross. He became sin for us so through faith in Him we are now righteous, our spirit is reborn. The story isn't over yet. Now the Lord will gently lead you from where you are to where He wants you to be. He will not require of you, what you cannot do. He will strengthen you and lead you one step at a time.

I remember something I saw on a Christian television program that touched me deeply. It was when I first became a Christian and had a long way to go. This woman being interviewed by the Christian host had a vision of Jesus. She saw Jesus at the top of a long staircase that went up to heaven. She thought to herself, "I have to get up to Jesus; I have to get up that staircase." She ran to the staircase to begin climbing, she started climbing with all her strength but before she got far at all she looked up and there was Jesus. He had climbed down to be with her.

Jesus is going to meet you where you are, and for most of us that is pretty messed up. We are all at different places when we come to the Lord. Some of us are in deep bondage to sin. We have come from deep places of darkness, and Satan has a stronghold. This is because some of us have deep damage to our souls through abuse or sins passed down through generational curses. On the other hand, some of us have been brought up in loving homes and have little damage to our souls. We all have different problems and needs. The Lord will deal with each of us differently. Remember this is in our souls; our spirits are made perfect through faith in Jesus.

God Looks at the Heart

We look at people and see a mess, we see their sin. Sin is a very bad thing and people that sin become miserable, but God does not expect immediate perfection from people. We don't say the sinner's prayer and then pop out perfect. There is a process that begins. It begins in the heart, in a place only God sees. He sees inside each heart and deals with each individual gently and lovingly.

Think of it this way, think of sin like an ocean. Some people come to God from a depth of fifty feet. This person, fifty feet deep in sin, comes to God and begins to swim up to the surface. They may move quickly, and they may move slowly, it depends on how much importance they have put on this new life they have begun. They may not even put much effort in at all but still they are with the Lord and at least they are floating upward. But all in all, it is good they are moving toward holiness, and they don't raise anyone's eyebrows because their life looks pretty good on the outside.

The next guy comes to the Lord, and he is coming from a depth of fifty thousand feet. Not only is he at the bottom of the ocean he is wrapped in seaweed. He has a lot farther to go than the last person. He is wrapped in guilt and shame, but he wants to serve the Lord, so he begins to swim upward. Even though he uses all his strength he doesn't move very fast because the weight of the seaweed is pulling down on him. Is he unacceptable to the Lord? No, no no! The Lord sees the whole picture; He sees the effort and the struggle. This man much deeper in sin is righteous to God. His swim to the surface may take years but he is righteous before God because God is looking at his heart.

A Woman's Finds Freedom God's Way

A close friend of mine, named Patty, had a long struggle with sin which for years she seemed to be losing. She had a deep problem with sin. She was into drugs and everything that went with them, including committing crimes and spending time in prison. She would come to the Lord and try to be perfect. She would throw out the drugs the cigarettes and the live-in boyfriend and she would go all out to do right. The problem was she wasn't strong enough. After a few days she would give up and she would be right back in her old life. After many years most everyone in her life gave up on her. She had even given up on herself. Someone begged her to go back to church on an Easter Sunday and she did. She gave her life to the Lord again, this time the Lord told her, "Don't change anything."

She didn't, she didn't throw out the boyfriend, she didn't quit smoking, she had successfully completed a drug rehab program, so she was free from that. God led her gently out of the sin she was in, over a period of years. He only required of her what she could handle. Now many years later she is still serving the Lord and she is one of the strongest Christians I have ever met. She is working on a book about her powerful story called *Out of the Depths*.

Her Heart Is Perfect

God values a perfect heart. It is more important to nurture a perfect heart in someone than to demand perfection from them. I remember learning this lesson one day.

My children did not have life easy. They grew up in an alcoholic home and they faced a lot of chaos. Because of this they could be very unruly. They did, however, all three of them have a relationship with the Lord.

Church was a challenge; they did not sit very still during the service. I remember one time when my daughter Lonna was ten years old, and we were in church. In fact, we were in church a lot because our church was having a revival meeting and holding services every day. My sister and her husband and their four children had driven down to Florida from Michigan to attend the revival with us.

I did not realize kids could be so good in church until we sat with her kids. Her kids sat quietly while mine went to the drinking fountain and the bathroom every few minutes. I got embarrassed. Lonna jumped up again to go to the drinking fountain and get another drink and I followed her out. I had enough. I caught hold of her in the hallway and told her I was going to spank her. I was mad and she was fixing to get it good. I turned her around and raised my arm to swat her; she held her breath and closed her eyes.

"Don't spank her!" I heard God's voice loudly and firmly. He continued. "Her heart is perfect toward me." Then He added, "Your children go through stress that most children don't go through, and their behavior can be worked on later when there is less stress, but for now leave her alone her heart is perfect."

We as Christians need to be careful who we spank. We can't go around spanking those whose hearts are perfect. Does that mean we lower the bar on sin? No, absolutely not. Jesus didn't, He raised the bar. We don't condone sin; our goal is to be free and to see others free. But if God only requires of us what we can handle at the time then who are we to demand perfection from our fellow Christians, or even from unbelievers. We need to remember that holiness is a delicate walk of faith and obedience, and it does take time.

Don't Be Deceived

There is always two sides to a pendulum. While some people feel they could never attain holiness and because they don't understand God's grace, they refuse to even try to become a Christian. Then there are those on the opposite end of the spectrum who feel that because they have been justified by faith they can go ahead, and sin and God will forgive them. This is called willfully sinning. This is not the same as those who are bound to sin and working with God toward freedom. What does scripture say?

What then? Shall we sin because we are not under the law but under grace? Certainly not! Do you not know that to whom you present yourselves slaves to obey you are that one's slaves whom you obey, whether of sin to death, or obedience to righteousness? Romans 6:15-16

The bottom line here is we should always be trying our best. We should obey God and not harden our hearts when He convicts us. When it comes to sin, we must be relentless, if we fail, we ask forgiveness and we pick ourselves up and try again. If we keep trying and don't give up, we will win.

Obey God's Word

People get into deception when it comes to sin because they want to do something wrong. You do not need a word from God if the Bible tells you something is wrong! You are not an exception to the rule, no one is.

Years ago, I met a couple from church, who were both married to other people. They met at church. Both the man and the woman had families. They divorced their spouses and left their children to be together.

What blew my mind was they told everyone it was God's will! I would see them at church meetings, and they would be the first ones to prophecy. They thought they were the exception to the rule, that they had God's blessing, that He had ordained their sin. They seemed to be at every meeting in town. They were actually encouraging others in the church to get a divorce.

I knew a woman who had recently had an affair and I was encouraging her to do the right thing and return to her husband. These two got a hold of her and encouraged her to marry the other man, that it was God's will.

Let me tell you something right now, God will not go against His word. The Bible is very clear on adultery, it is very clear on a lot of sins. If you are engaging in sin and you think God says it is okay and that you are the exception to the rule, you have been deceived. We are to be obedient to God and obedient to scripture. If the Bible says it is wrong, then it is wrong.

We have a commandment from the Lord to be holy. We are to do our best. When we fail, we will repent and try again; knowing Jesus our High Priest has made atonement for us. He will lead us and guide us; He will not require more of us than we can handle. We are not to deceive ourselves and say sin isn't sin. When we sin, we will admit it and confess it and ask Him for his help. If we are trapped in sin, He will bring us out. We are not to judge another's progress. Remember sin is more than just bad habits. Sin is also things that are unseen like unforgiveness, anger, bitterness and unbelief.

We all have a long way to go. We will get there. Be humble. Be quick to repent. Be determined. Allow God to work in your heart. Don't give up on yourself. Don't condemn yourself or others. You are holy now, through the blood of Jesus, by faith. You are like an apple growing on a tree. You are not ripe yet, you are still green, you are not sweet you are sour, but you are perfect, the sweetness will come, the ripeness will come. You are abiding on the vine {Jesus is the vine} the life from the vine is growing you and maturing you.

You will be holy just as Jesus is holy, you are going through a process and you are being prepared for eternity, an eternity of holiness.

Chapter Twelve
Who is Jesus?

I am the Alpha and the Omega, the Beginning and the End the First and the Last. Revelation 22:13

Who is Jesus? Who is He that we should follow His example?

Jesus is eternal. He has always existed. He is the Beginning and the End. Jesus is God. God is made up of the Father, Jesus and the Holy Spirit. They are three but they are One. God created us as we see in Genesis, which includes all of the Godhead, Father, Son and Holy Spirit, working together. Although we are told in scripture that Jesus was called the Word.

In the beginning was the Word, and the Word was with God, and the Word was God. He was in the beginning with God. All things were made through Him and without Him nothing was made that was made. In Him was life and the life was light of men. John1:1-4

Jesus Is Our Creator

Jesus is our creator and nothing has been made without Him. All life comes from Him. You are an expression of Jesus. He is your creator and He is the life within you. You exist because of Him and by Him. The Father, Jesus and the Holy Spirit are three distinct personalities, but they operate as One. Jesus said it this way.

"He who has seen Me has seen the Father; so how can you say show us the Father? Do you not believe that I am in the Father and the Father in Me? The words that I speak to you I do not speak on My own authority; but the Father who dwells in Me does the works. Believe Me that I am the Father and the Father in Me, or else believe Me for the sake of the works themselves."

I remember when I was fifteen years old. I was sitting in the bathroom. I had only been saved for a year and I was thinking to myself that I was not going to make it. The Lord Jesus spoke to me, as He heard my thoughts. His voice sounded audible. He said, "I will take you every step of the way."

I remember thinking to myself after He spoke. I know that voice, it is part of me. I have been hearing it my whole life but didn't realize it. I recognized it when I heard it audibly. It was a familiar sounding voice, closer than my mother, closer than my twin sister, part of me. That is because His voice is the voice of my creator. I have come forth from Him. I love that voice with all my being, I long to hear that voice again.

Jesus is the only One anywhere that truly knows you. Even you do not truly know yourself as Jesus knows you. He formed you, designed you, He knows your strengths and weaknesses. He knows your future, your past, and He is there. He is ahead of you, and He is behind you. He is always with you. Nothing can exist without Him and that includes you. Aren't you glad that He loves you?

Jesus and the Father are One

Back to the trinity. Spiritual things can be hard for our minds to comprehend. The trinity is one of those things. I like the way Jesse Duplantis described Jesus and the Father as being one, in his book, *Heaven Close Encounters of the God Kind.* This book tells of Jesse's experience in Heaven in August of 1988. Part of Jesse's experience takes place before the throne of God the Father. He describes it beautifully. Jesse is lying on the floor in front of the Throne of God.

Everything in heaven is beautiful. The floor looked like marble with gold in it, gold thread or veins running through the marble. Although I couldn't look up for a very long time, I looked up from the floor in the direction of the overwhelming light, and I saw Him! I saw Elohim, Jehovah God, Yahweh sitting on the throne! But I saw His feet- only His feet. The light was so bright that came from Him, I couldn't see His face. Now I know why the scripture says we can't see Jehovah's face and live- at least I know I couldn't. I had to keep looking down the

light was so intense. But I looked again, and I saw the lower part of His hand resting on the arm of the Throne. He is so big you can't describe Him in a dimension. His hand is huge! His body, the form of it, is sort of like energy, spirit. There is a wall around the Throne, but the Throne is higher than the wall- that's why you can see the Throne from every direction, from a distance. And that power, that energy-like smoke of God, covers all around the chair of the Throne itself.

I heard a sound, *Whoooooosh!*. There was a massive amount of energy in that place. That's the only way I can explain it. It was God's power! You hear that noise, then the energy goes back into Him. There is smoke and power and noise—the place is noisy! And angels are hollering.

I was still lying on my face and getting weaker. In that mass of energy and power I could see God, Jehovah—His feet—sitting. There is a huge platform in front of the Throne like a stage. It seemed level to me but actually it was raised. The topography of the land goes up toward the Throne. Then out of that massive energy of Light and love and power I saw Jesus come in human form. There He was, like I had seen him in Paradise. What seemed to be millions of people at the Throne of God fell down before Him. For the first time in my life, I could understand the Trinity in physical terms. Jesus came out of that cloud and the power of the Father. Jesus literally came out of the very existence of Jehovah God, and when He did the people shouted. Jesus and the Father were One, yet They were Two. He was in the Father and the Father was in Him. He was at the right

hand of God. When He came out of that power He was in human form- something we could touch.

I like hearing Jesse's description of what he saw in heaven. It gives us a picture of Jesus' words when He said that He and the Father are one. It also gives us a picture of how awesome it is to stand or as Jesse was doing, to lay before the throne of God. I am looking forward to being there someday and seeing for myself.

Jesus is Our Redeemer

So, who is Jesus? He became a man, but He was not a man. He was the Word, the Creator of the world. He became the Son of God, but He was not the Son of God, He became the Son of God to redeem us.

He is so much more than we realize, than is possible to realize. Because He is the force by which all things are held together. He is the force by which everything you see is held together, including you. Can you try to wrap your head around it?

He is more. The wind obeyed Him, the seas obeyed Him, He recreated arms and legs and eyeballs, because He has command over every bit of matter. He knows all He sees all, He fills all things. There is a giant force field called the universe which is gigantic and full of energy and power that goes for billions of light years in every direction. He is that force.

He is God, He is eternal, and He is our creator.

What else? Jesus is our Redeemer, our Mediator between us and God the Father. Jesus is our Salvation. His coming to earth in human form, His life, His death on a cross and His resurrection had a huge purpose for you. Our greatest need, although many don't even realize it, is for a Redeemer. Jesus has become our Redeemer. Jesus is the one and only way to God. In Jesus is hope and He is our only hope. This is where we differ from all the other religions. Jesus is the only way to God. *John 14:6 Jesus said to him, "I am the way the truth and the life. No one comes to the Father except through Me."*

If you don't realize the importance of Jesus to you, right now, the day will come when you will. Those who have rejected Jesus have no hope. They are eternally hopeless. I don't even like to think of such things, it is to awful for words.

Why should we follow Jesus?

I think of the time in the Bible when many of the disciples of Jesus deserted Him. *John 6:66-68 From that time many of His disciples went back and walked with Him no more. Then Jesus asked the twelve, "Do you also want to walk away?" Then Simon Peter answered Him, "Lord to whom shall we go? You have the words of eternal life."*

Why should we follow Jesus?

Who else is there?

Jesus is Life, without Him is death, I want to follow Him.

Jesus is Light without Him there is darkness, I want to follow Him.

I exist through Him, I overcome through Him, I have hope through Him.
He gives me peace when I am afraid, when I call, He answers, He guides me, He protects me, He provides for me.

When no one else cared He cared. He loves me like no other. He has saved me and rescued me, He died for me. To whom shall we go? He has the words of life.

Chapter Thirteen

Why Did Jesus Come?

"No one has ascended to heaven but He who came down from heaven, that is the Son of Man who is in heaven. And as Moses lifted the serpent in the wilderness, even so the Son of Man must be lifted up, that whoever believes in Him should not perish but have eternal life. For God so loved the world He gave His only begotten Son, that whoever believes in Him should not perish but have everlasting life. For God didn't send His Son into the world to condemn the world, but that the world through Him might be saved."

John 3:13-16   Jesus' first purpose for coming to earth was to redeem mankind. Our salvation was His primary purpose for coming to earth. Jesus' death on a cross and resurrection, is the most significant event not only in the history of earth, but also for all eternity. The greatest event to ever have happened, ever, was the sacrifice of Jesus. Jesus came and did this for us.

The Highest Priority, The Blood of Jesus

The blood of Jesus is the most holy, most sacred priority of God. The Jews celebrated this event for thousands of years before it happened in the Passover. This was the first feast of the Jews ever celebrated and it was celebrated on the evening before Moses led them out of Egypt. It was all symbolic of what was to come.

The Jews sacrificed a lamb and spread its blood on the top and either side of their doorpost. Interesting isn't it, they made a cross of blood on their door. Then they were led out of Egypt, through the Red Sea and were led through the wilderness by the cloud and the fire until they reached the Promised Land. This is all represents our salvation, the blood of Jesus on the door of our hearts, our freedom from slavery to sin, is symbolized by the Israelites coming out of Egypt, and baptism is symbolized by their passing through the Red Sea. Then there is the cloud and the fire representing our following the Holy Spirit who is present with us on earth now until we reach the Promised Land, heaven. The blood of Jesus, the greatest priority of God and man, was celebrated many years before it came to pass.

Communion

Now we celebrate this event with communion. We drink the grape juice and eat the piece of bread in remembrance of the most important event not only for all mankind but for each of us personally. The grape juice represents His blood, the bread his broken body. The event of Jesus death and resurrection is not only the most important eternal event, the most important historical event but also the most important event in your own life. It all comes down to you and what you will do with it. Will you receive it?

Communion is such a special time. It is powerful. It is powerful because it represents the most significant event, ever. As we take communion, we are celebrating that we personally have received the blood of Jesus, and we have become one of the redeemed.

We are remembering what the most important thing in our life is, and that is to receive the gift of the blood of Jesus which is the only hope we have to redeem our eternal souls; we are lining up our priorities as we take it.

A Special Memory of Communion for Summer

One communion time was very special and became very personal to me. It was when I was a young wife and new mother, about twenty-three years old. I was going through a very difficult time in my life. I felt worthless.

I had always struggled with feelings that I was not good enough and that I had no right to be here on earth. Now, early in my marriage, those feelings had gotten even worse. We were at the bottom financially. We didn't have enough money to pay our bills, we barely had food, I was wearing the same dress every day because I couldn't fit into my pre-baby clothes and I had no money for clothes, much less a haircut and I looked miserable.

My marriage had been harder than I could have

possibly dreamed it would be and I felt we together were worthless along with our babies. My being unable to make it as an adult had accentuated my feelings that I always had, that I was worthless and just a big mistake.

Here we were sitting at church, and I felt I had no right to be there with all these other normal people. Life worked for them. They all seemed to be doing fine. They all seemed to be able to survive and belong on this planet, but it wasn't that way for me. I felt like a weed in the middle of a flower garden. For some reason coming to church would bring all these feelings to the surface and I would cry all through church.

This morning was no different. I was sitting in church barely looking up, with tears streaming down my face. It was time for communion, and the Pastor told us to prepare our hearts to take it. I tried to, but I felt so miserable I couldn't pray. As I sat holding my tiny cup of grape juice, I decided to close my eyes and just picture Jesus on the cross, instead.

My heart was so full of pain, that pain was easy to picture. I easily pictured Jesus in agony on the cross in front of me. Though my eyes were closed, I was intently looking at Jesus, suffering there before me; it was almost like I was there. As I felt such agony in my heart, I was witnessing His on the cross. We were silently suffering together as I gazed upward at Jesus, from the foot of the cross.

And then as I was looking, a large drop of blood formed on His brow. I watched.

Suddenly it dropped from His face and landed in my communion cup. It landed with a little splash.

I gasped.

It was so real that it startled me, and I opened my eyes. I looked down in my little communion cup I was holding in my lap. That was Jesus blood in there, it was a drop of Jesus blood, I saw it fall in there! I actually had a drop of His blood!

Then I looked up, around the room. And everyone's communion cup stood out. I saw a sea of communion cups around the room. They were in each person's hands. One drop was in each cup. It suddenly dawned on me that we all had an equal portion. We each had the same portion of Jesus blood. We were all equal. I realized I had the same worth of each person in that room; I had an equal portion of the blood of Jesus.

I sat there amazed.

You see, the sacrifice of Jesus, is the most important event in my life. It is personal. It gives me worth. Actually, it gives us everything. That one drop of blood is better than all the money in the world. It buys something that money can't. It is my every need met. It redeems my soul, it heals my body, it heals my mind, it also gives me access to the very throne of God. With it I can come before the Father in heaven, knowing that I belong there, I can come boldly, I can speak with Him, because of this one drop of blood.

It is priceless.

It is mine.

Jesus Came for You

Jesus came to earth for you, to shed His blood for

you, to purchase you. Not only that, but Jesus will also come to you whenever you need Him. He will always be there for you; He has been for me. He came to me when I was fourteen years old and told me He loved me. That is when I gave my heart to Him.

There were two times in my life that I was in such distress I actually went into shock and lost consciousness, both times I heard his voice audibly and that brought me back, just knowing He was there, right there with me, this gave me strength to go on.

One time I was in a spiritual battle with the devil, and he told me he was taking me to hell. I thought I was going but suddenly Jesus was there, I had no idea He had come because He was invisible, but when I needed Him, He came, I heard Him rebuke the devil and the devil left.

I have almost been in car accidents, but an invisible force stopped them, this has happened three times. He came. Why? Am I special, well yes, I am to Him but so are you, Jesus came to earth two thousand years ago, for you and He still comes every time we need Him.

This is the reason Jesus came.
Jesus came and He comes, He comes for you!

Chapter Fourteen

Following Jesus

Therefore we also, since we are surrounded by so great a cloud of witnesses, let us lay aside every weight, and the sin which so easily ensnares us, and let us run with endurance the race that is set before us, looking unto Jesus the author and finisher of our faith, who for the joy that was set before Him endured the cross, despising the shame and has sat down at the right hand of the throne of God.
Hebrews 12:1-3

The writer of Hebrews is writing to us about our race, or our life on earth, or even I guess we could say our journey with God while here on earth. Jesus, the author and finisher of our faith, ran it first, and now He has sat down at the right hand of the throne of God. Now it is our turn. As we run, we need to lay aside every weight, that means get rid of sin; we don't need anything weighing us down or ensnaring us and follow this trail Jesus blazed for us. We look unto Him. Where does it lead? It leads us to the throne of God, to the pinnacle, the absolute apex of the entire universe, where Jesus is seated at the right hand of God.

Laying Aside the Weights

Following Jesus is an adventure!

As we run the race set before us the road behind us should become littered with the things we no longer need. Pride will be dropped and unforgiveness, these things are too heavy to carry, as we follow our example Jesus, as we run this race that is set before us. Things we used to do will no longer appeal to us as we fix our eyes on Jesus. Worldly attractions lose their hold. Our speech changes, we no longer use our words to hurt people but to build them up. We become increasingly uncomfortable with idle speech or carelessly using words.

What is happening? Our image is being changed. We are starting to look like Jesus on the inside. We are being filled on the inside with light and love and peace. We no longer need the accolades of men, somehow it doesn't matter so much what people think and we no longer fear them. We fear God, we want more of Him and now we care what He thinks. We are changing, in our thoughts, in our actions, how we spend our money, how we spend our time, how we treat others. We are becoming less self-centered, and more Christ centered.

Summer Learns a Lesson from Her Children

It was so important to me to teach my children about the Lord and not only that, but for them to have a relationship with Jesus for themselves. Well, my son, my oldest became a Christian at the age of three, my two daughters were younger than he. What I didn't know was that they could, as children, follow the Lord so much better than I. I had never had the courage to talk to others about my faith. I was afraid of people and painfully shy; this is still a major issue with me. My three-year-old son started telling everyone he met about Jesus. He didn't learn it from me. He told strangers on the street, families taking picnics on our daily walks to the park, a little old lady who he passed, rebellious teenaged boys, and even my mother-in-law! I had never been able to share my faith and my three-year-old was doing it! He was following Jesus for himself.

My girls were just as amazing, my youngest daughter, Joy taught me so much about selflessness and love. She as a little child would help me on my newspaper route. It was a very difficult thing to do. I would have to get up about one thirty in the morning, after only a few hours of sleep and get up and go deliver nearly five hundred papers. My little girl, Joy, age seven, didn't want me to go alone, she would make herself wake up and come and then she would work like a grown up, because she loved me, she never even asked for money, and I don't think I ever paid her. She did it out of love. She would amaze me with her love for others. It was very hard for her, and she needed her sleep, but she would shake herself awake and go with me for no other reason but love for me. Her sister, Lonna, was also an example to me. During a financial emergency when I had to take on extra work, she helped me deliver two thousand phone books.

A couple of times I was put to shame by my children's Christ like example, and I realized   I would have to change and stop being so selfish. The first incident was when we went to a fair at a church. My daughter, Joy and I both won a cake in the cake walk. These weren't regular cakes; these were church lady home baked cakes, the kind you eat once in a lifetime. Mine was a red cake with thick white frosting covered in pecans! And it was huge. I felt like I had won the lottery. I just wanted to go home and eat it! Joy also, to her delight, won a cake. This is when she was about seven or eight years old. We were both excitedly clutching our cakes as we arrived home. My only thought was a fork!

Suddenly, as we pulled into our driveway, Joy remembered it was Mr. York's birthday. He was a little old man who was ailing and lived next door to us! Her cake never made it in the door; she went straight to Mr. York's house with her cake. It made her so happy to give it to him for his birthday. I wouldn't have parted with my cake for anything; I wondered how she could be so loving! I realized, just how far I had to go to be Christ-like.

About three years later, I realized I still hadn't come very far. This time it was a tubing trip. Our family had a new hobby, tubing down the nearby river in inner tubes. Our family really got into it so I went out and bought each of us nice tubes and we went whenever we could. We had a special place went to upriver and we would float down river and get out at a park. The whole thing took about two hours to do and once we got started there was no turning back, we would leave one car two hours down river and drive another up to the starting point.

It was some of the most fun we ever had. We had special spots along the river we would especially enjoy, there was a deep spot to swim and an old bridge to climb up and do a high jump into the water, and even a spot where a tree fell down that we liked to climb and to jump off. It was my favorite thing to do so whenever I could, we would go. That was the reason I invested in good inner-tubes.

One day my sister and her kids decided to go with us. Well, we got about ten minutes down river and my little niece started crying because her tube wasn't very big, and she was sinking.

I remember thinking to myself, "They should have bought her a decent tube, I am not giving up my tube!" I felt irritated.

Joy, on the other hand, immediately jumped off her tube and traded with her cousin. She didn't give it a second thought. She joyfully made the two-hour trip on a sinking tube and she never complained, she made the best of it.

I remember thinking that day, "I have to change." That day was a turning point for me. I purposed to stop living so selfishly. My children followed Jesus much better than I, and I wanted to change, I wanted to stop being so selfish and be more Christ-like.

Following Jesus Every Day

Following Jesus is more than just following the Bible, it is following the living Christ who has made His home inside your heart. It is a daily choice to give your life to Him and follow Him.

I have to tell you in my life following Jesus has not been glamorous. It is seeing Him in others, in your children, in your husband, and in those around you and giving them your best. It has looked more like hard work. It looked like changing diapers, laundry and three meals a day; it looked like washing dishes and sitting up nights with sick children. It looked like putting others needs before my own, daily for years on end. It looked like forgiving my husband over and over and over every time he would start drinking again or lose another job. It looked like putting one foot in front of another one day at a time. It meant trusting the Lord that even though the path I was on seemed to be endless and certainly not glamorous, and difficult, I was being formed into His image as I traveled down it. I had to set my face as a flint; I had to keep going when I felt things were hopeless.

I have learned something. Ordinary, everyday lives, what we call the grey days, are important. Everyday faithfulness, everyday obedience, being faithful to God and to those around us is what builds our spiritual house on the rock, as Jesus taught in the Sermon on the Mount. When the storms of life come, and they come, those who have built their house on a rock will stand out above the others.

No One Is Invisible to God

Let's talk about Angelo again, the homeless man, that we talked about in chapter eight who became a mighty king in heaven. His life seemed to be insignificant to those on earth. He was born deaf and was unloved by his parents. He could not speak. He was abused, not only by his parents but also in the facility he was placed in by the authorities. As an adult he was turned out onto the streets and homeless. He is unknown, unseen and insignificant. He has fallen through the cracks of our society and at first, he steals to live.

But we learn he uses everything God has placed in him, all the shares of love, to use the exact wording, to overcome. He stops stealing even though it means he almost starves to death.

This may seem small, but it isn't. Although no one on earth knows Angelo exists, all of heaven is watching. He has touched the heart of Almighty God. He unknowingly is being watched by a great crowd in heaven, they see him go further. He finds a gospel tract and gives his heart to the Lord. Now he spends half of his meager income to buy gospel tracts and hand them out on the street corner. He actually leads one man to the Lord. Now, he would stand there for the rest of his life just to lead someone else to the Lord.

He is still unknown on earth but in heaven a great crowd has gathered, the great crowd of witnesses, their excitement has risen to such a peak they have jumped to their feet, and they are cheering him on! They have seen the Father God's heart touched, and this excites them too. No sport arena on earth has ever seen such excitement. This man is running the race and following Jesus with such determination and such endurance as heaven has ever seen.

An unknown man, whose home is a cardboard box, has caught the attention of God Himself and has all the saints in heaven cheering. Finally, they cry out to God to bring him home to heaven, to his reward. Angelo's life didn't look like much here, on earth, but all of heaven noticed. Now he is a great king. He found he had a huge family when he got to heaven that had rejoiced at his life lived for God.

I want you to remember, when you start following Jesus, when you begin to love those around you, and forgive those who hurt you and to bless your enemies, when you begin to use all your effort, when you begin to run and lay down everything, and run with endurance the race set before you, when you begin to choose the narrow path, and begin to live like Jesus, you may not be cheered on or even noticed on earth. But God who sees your heart will stand up and take notice! He sees that you are trying, you may even fail but you get back up and you try again. You take a step toward God, and you take another step before God and now you're starting to run just a little, then pretty soon you take off and give God all you have, you put all your effort into running toward Him, and God has taken notice of you, He stands up and He is moved. Now all those in heaven see you too, and they are watching with interest. An obstacle comes your way, but you endure, you don't stop. Now they stand up and cheer. You are known in heaven. Your life on earth may or may not change, you may feel invisible, but you are not invisible to God. He sees, He takes notice, and He is waiting for you at the finish line! Not only is your Father there but so is Jesus who ran first and all those who followed, they are cheering you on and waiting there for you.

Who Can Run the Race?

My children started running the race at ages two and three. Angelo ran his race with no education and no money and no one to help him, not even the church. You are never too poor or too rich, too old or too young, too smart or too stupid, too ugly or too pretty, too fat or too skinny. It is never too early or too late to start as long as you are alive. Fix your eyes on Jesus the author and finisher of your faith. Listen to Him, follow Him, obey Him, and live like He did.

Don't Get Weary

If you're in this race and you have gotten tired, I can relate. It is time to lay aside these weights I have picked up again. It is hard to run carrying the cares of this life. I will have to put them down again. The tired can run this race also. We just need to get moving again. Start choosing the narrow path again, the Bible instead of the television set, time with God instead of sleep and obedience when He calls.

The Path May Get Difficult but Jesus Goes with You

Jesus leads us, but that means He is going with us and He goes first. He is your provider and defender on this journey.

He may lead you through the desert, but He will give you water from the rock on the journey. He may lead you through the valley of the shadow of death, but He will never leave you, and the green pastures and still waters are coming. He may lead you on a path that seems to be a dead end, but the sea will part for you.

There are miracles on this path, you may walk on water or still a storm or heal the sick or raise the dead!

It may lead to a cross and a tomb but there will also be a resurrection.

Jesus is the way. The path will always lead you from darkness to light, from bondage to freedom, always higher, always closer to God.

The life you live will also destroy the works of darkness and will also set others free, just as Jesus' did. You will bring hope to others and make the way easier for those who come behind you, just as others have followed Jesus and made the way easier before us. Those whose names we know and those whose names we don't know. Let us join them who have also followed and run their race, let us follow the One who has gone before us and made the way, our example, JESUS!

Epilogue

I want to end this book with a very special invitation to anyone who may have read this book but hasn't begun the journey of following Jesus. Are you still on the wide road that leads to destruction? Would you like to follow Jesus down a different road, it is much narrower, but it leads to Life. This is the fork in the road for you. Will you change paths? I promise you it will be the best thing you ever do. It was for me. Let's simply pray the prayer given by the Chinese orphan in chapter five.

The Chinese orphan boy said to get down on your knees and pray. Say…. "Jesus, I am a sinner. I was on my road to hell. I am fit only for hell. The big load I carry is sin. Forgive my sins and teach me to live only for your glory. Amen"

Now, follow Jesus, He is your example.

Notes

Chapter Two .... *The Final Quest*, by Rick Joyner, copyright 1996 used by permission, www.morningstarministries.org

Chapter Three.......*Heaven, Close Encounters of the God Kind,* by Jesse Duplantis
           Harrison House, Tulsa Oklahoma
           pages 93-94
Angels on Assignment, by Roland H. Buck Hunter Books Houston, Texas pages 41-42

Chapter Five.......... *The Heavens Opened* by Anna Rountree Creation House
           Lake Mary, Florida Page 60

Chapter Six...........*Visions beyond the Veil,* by H. A. Baker Whitaker House
           Springdale, Pennsylvania
           Pages 91-92

The Call, by Rick Joyner copyright 1999 used by permission www,morningstarministries,org

The Guideposts Treasury of Love, Guideposts Carmel, New York   Pages 278-280

Chapter Seven………. *The Archko Volume*,
translated by Drs. McIntosh and Twyman
Mc Graw Hill   pages 83, 84, 85

God Calling, edited by A.J. Russell Jove Publications
          New York, New York

Chapter Eight….*The Archko Volume*, translated by
Drs. McIntosh and Twyman McGraw Hill
          Page 84

The Final Quest, by Rick Joyner, copyright 1996,
used by permission,
www.morningstarministries.org

Chapter Nine…*One Man's Faith and Miracles*,
by Alvin "Mike" Martin
Kings Press, Seattle, Washington
          Page 84-87

Chapter Ten…*Mountain Moving Faith*,
          by Kenneth E. Hagin   Faith Library
Publications Tulsa, Oklahoma
          Pages 13-14

Chapter Twelve.
          Heaven, Close Encounters of the God Kind,
          by Jesse Duplantis
          Harrison House, Tulsa, Oklahoma
                    Pages   113-115

www.ingramcontent.com/pod-product-compliance
Lightning Source LLC
LaVergne TN
LVHW011232080426
835509LV00005B/462